D1194387

Ideology

Second Edition

Concepts in Social Thought

Series Editor: Frank Parkin

Concepts in Social Thought

Ideology

Second Edition

David McLellan

University of Minnesota Press
Minneapolis

Copyright 1995 David McLellan

All rights reserved. No part of this publication may be reproduced,
stored in a retrieval system, or transmitted, in any form or by
any means, electronic, mechanical, photocopying, recording, or
otherwise, without the prior written permission of the publisher.

First published in this second edition by Open University Press, 1995

·Published simultaneously in the United States, 1995
by the University of Minnesota Press
111 Third Avenue South, Suite 290
Minneapolis, MN 55401-2520

Printed in Great Britain

Library of Congress Cataloging-in-Publication Data
McLellan, David.
 Ideology / David McLellan. — 2nd ed.
  p.   cm. — (Concepts in social thought)
  Includes bibliographical references (p.   ) and index.
  ISBN 0-8166-2802-5 (hc)   ISBN 0-8166-2803-3 (pbk.)
  1. Ideology — History. I. Title. II. Series.
JA83.M35   1995
320.5 — dc20   95-16276

The University of Minnesota is an
equal-opportunity educator and employer.

For Oliver

Contents

Preface

This small book is intended to be no more than the briefest of introductions to an extremely slippery subject. The topic is as wide as it is fundamental to the social sciences and I am well aware of my being able merely to touch the surface. But I hope at least to stimulate the reader's interest and I have therefore added a detailed list of further reading and an extensive bibliography. I am grateful to Jean Gil, Gabrielle McLellan, Stephanie McLellan, Gay Mitchell, and Keith Webb who have all helped to improve the book.

David McLellan

Preface to the Second Edition

In an effort to keep up with the continuing vagaries of ideology, I have thoroughly revised the text, added a new chapter, and considerably expanded both the Further Reading and the Bibliography.

David McLellan

The Career of a Concept

Ideology is the most elusive concept in the whole of social science. For it asks about the bases and validity of our most fundamental ideas. As such, it is an essentially contested concept, that is, a concept about the very definition (and therefore application) of which there is acute controversy.[1]

With significant exceptions, the word ideology comes trailing clouds of pejorative connotation. Ideology is someone *else's* thought, seldom our own. That our thought might be ideological is a suggestion that we almost instinctively reject lest the foundations of our most cherished conceptions turn out to be composed of more shifting sand than we would like. Therefore, the history of the concept of ideology is the history of various attempts to find a firm Archimedean point outside the sphere of ideological discourse, an immoveable spot from which to observe the levers of ideology at work. In the main Marxist tradition this point has consisted in the search for a particular group or class whose representatives would have a peculiar vocation for non-ideological thought. In the Enlightenment, rationalist, empiricist tradition, trust has been placed in an objective science of society which would unmask the irrationality of ideological conceptions. Both traditions envisage the possibility of a society without ideology - whether a Marxist society where ideology seen as a bulwark of class power will no longer be necessary or a capitalist society where the self-evident norms of a rational market economy will impose themselves. But the spectre of the relativism of all claims to truth which has plagued humankind, at least since Plato's Protagoras denied the possibility of objective truth, refuses to be laid. Any examination of ideology makes it difficult to avoid the rueful conclusion that all views about ideology are themselves ideological. But avoided it must be – or at least modified by saying that some views are more ideological than others. For the simple thought that all views are ideological encounters two difficulties: first, that it borders on the vacuous, since it is so all-embracing as to be almost meaningless; second and more damagingly, it contains the same logical absurdity as the declaration of Epimenides the Cretan who declared that all Cretans were liars. A more discriminating approach is therefore necessary not only intellectually but also practically: we are indeed all implicated in ideology which is both real and powerful[2]; but an understanding of this fact can at least prevent us from becoming its unconscious victims.

Unlike many other similarly controversial terms (democracy, say, or liberty), ideology is less than 200 years old. It is the product of the social, political and intellectual upheavals that accompanied the Industrial Revolution: the spread of democratic ideals, the politics of mass movements, the idea that, since we have made the world, we can also remake it. According to the German social philosopher Jurgen Habermas, these new world-views

> emerge from the critique of dogmatism of traditional interpretations of the world and claim a scientific character. Yet they retain legitimating functions, thereby keeping actual power relations inaccessible to analysis and to public consciousness. It is in this way that ideologies in the restricted sense first came into being. They replace traditional legitimations of power by appearing in the mantle of modern science and by deriving their justification from the critique of ideology. Ideologies are coeval with the critique of ideology. In this sense there can be no pre-bourgeois ideologies.[3]

Traditional beliefs, just because they are traditional, tend to be static and to rely on a restricted, hierarchically structured, coherent entities: myths did not compete. Ideologies, on the other hand, were the products of an increasingly pluralist society and were associated with rival groups whose sectional interests they served.[4] Whereas traditional religion concentrated on the interaction between the everyday life of individuals and the sacredness of an other-worldly dimension, the secularized universe of ideology concerned itself with public projects of this-worldly transformation to be legitimized by apparently self-justifying appeals to science and to reason. The organizing myths of past societies were inherited and constituted a given framework that transcended the social world; ideologies are typically our own creation drawn from painstaking investigations of our own societies. This tendency is, in turn, enhanced by the increased democratization of the political process. The industrial revolution involved also a communications revolution in which literacy expended enormously in parallel with the unprecedented cheapness of books and newspapers. The increase in information available and the fact that it issued from highly divergent sources meant that its interpretation became problematic and competing frameworks, reflecting different interests, emerged to make sense of all the new material. But these frameworks, or ideologies, in spite of their inevitably partial origin, had to have a universal appeal. For with the increased participation of the masses in politics, persuasion rather than mere command was the order of the day. In the age of liberty, fraternity and equality, the only approaches that could even aspire to universal acceptance were those based on the apparently universal ideas of reason and science, of which Francis Fukayama's work is but the latest example.[5]

Like so many other enticing things, the word ideology is of French origin. But although directly a product of the French Enlightenment, the notion obviously has its roots in the general philosophical questions about meaning and direction with which the breakdown of the medieval world view confronted Western European intellectuals. These questions were encouraged by the impact of Protestantism with its insistence on the individual, on liberty of conscience, and on the transformative power of the word rather than the reassuring presence of ritual. More direct precursors, however, of the original discussants of ideology, were thinkers such as Francis Bacon and Thomas Hobbes. In his *Novum Organon* (1620) Bacon attempted to outline an approach to the study of society based on observation. Hitherto, human understanding had been obscured by what he called idols – mistaken, irrational conceptions. There were four sorts of idol: idols of the tribe, idols of the cave, idols of the market place, and idols of the theatre. The first idols, those of the tribe, include the tendency to accept what has been hallowed by tradition or to let the passions interfere with the acquisition of rational knowledge. The idols of the cave are those which arise from the particular viewpoint of the individual which often precludes a more general perspective. The idols of the market place are linguistic, the market place being the symbol for social interaction which is often at variance with reality and thus, again, an obstruction to rational understanding. The idols of the theatre are the dogmatic conceptions of former times which, given the absence of any empirical foundation, are no better than dramatic fictions.

The Baconian theory of idols lies at the origin of modern social science. It strongly influenced both the English empirical tradition in Hobbes and Locke and the French Enlightenment which eventually produced the concept of ideology. Unlike their predecessors in England, where the power of throne and altar had been considerably curtailed in the previous century, the philosophers of the French Enlightenment had to contend with an absolutist monarchy in alliance with an autocratic church. Consequently, whereas for Machiavelli and Bacon religion had been a potentially integrating force, for the leading Enlightenment thinkers in France it was the chief obstacle to a rational ordering of society. The keys to this social reformation lay in reason and nature. As Holbach, one of their leading spokesmen, wrote:

> The source of man's unhappiness is his ignorance of nature. . . . The most important of our duties, then, is to seek means by which we may destroy delusions than can never do more than mislead us. The remedies for these evils must be sought for in Nature herself; it is only in the abundance of her resources, that we can rationally expect to find antidotes to the mischiefs brought upon us by an ill-directed, by an overpowering enthusiasm. . . . For this purpose reason must be restored to its proper rank. . . . It must no longer be held down by the massive chains of prejudice.[6]

The solution to the prejudices and lies fostered by priests and kings to bolster their own power lay in the omnipotence of education. Occasionally, Enlightenment thinkers admitted the social determinants of knowledge, as when Helvetius pointed out that insects living on grass eaten by sheep were liable to look on the sheep as ferocious predators but on the wolves, who preyed on the sheep, as entirely beneficent. But in general they had little defence against Marx's subsequent complaint that 'the materialist doctrine concerning the changing of circumstances and upbringing forgets that circumstances are changed by men and that it is essential to educate the educator himself'.[7] Their only reply was to place unlimited confidence in the power of reason to discredit prejudice.

Th? Enlightenment thinkers were the intellectual precursors of the French Revolution of 1789; and it was in the immediate aftermath of the French Revolution that the term ideology was first coined. Its originator, in 1797, was Antoine Destutt de Tracy, one of a group of philosophers whom the revolutionary Convention had put in charge of the newly founded Institut de France specifically to spread the ideas of the Enlightenment. The Institut briefly enjoyed the patronage of Napoleon, who became an honorary member before his Concordat with the Church and his growing personal despotism caused a breach. In his *Elements d'Ideologie*, written between 1801 and 1815, de Tracy proposed a new science of ideas, an idea-logy, which would be the ground of all other sciences. Rejecting the concept of innate ideas, de Tracy explained how all our ideas are based on physical sensations. A rational investigation of the origin of ideas, free from religious or metaphysical prejudice, would be the foundation of a just and happy society. For the investigation of individual ideas would show their common origin in universal human needs and desires. Those needs would form the framework of laws regulating society on a natural basis and promoting the harmonious fulfilment of the relevant desires. For the natural and the social coincided. And this coincidence would be laid bare by the rational assessment of the origin of ideas, by ideology.

Thus, in its origin, the notion of ideology was positive and progressive. In the eyes of Napoleon, however, it quickly became pejorative. As his government evolved towards an empire supported by established religion, criticism from the liberal and republican ideologues (as they came to be called) became inevitable. And it was partly them that Napoleon blamed after his retreat from Moscow:

> It is to ideology, this cloudy metaphysics which, by subtly searching for first causes, wishes to establish on this basis the legislation of peoples, instead of obtaining its laws from knowledge of the human heart and from the lessons of history, that we must attribute all the misfortunes of our fair France.[8]

This oscillation between a positive and a negative connotation will be characteristic of the whole history of the concept of ideology.

Ideology has a German, as well as a French, origin – though here, too, the French Revolution was a crucial event. For the Enlightenment philosophers, the principles on which they criticized the *ancien régime* and in the name of which the French Revolution was made, were self-evident. However, the aftermath of the French Revolution – Napoleon's rise to power and the cataclysmic events in Europe during the following two decades – seemed neither particularly natural nor rational. Moreover, the gathering pace of the Industrial Revolution put change and development at the very centre of the age. The Romantic movement, particularly strong in Germany, laid emphasis on the way in which we invest the world with our own meanings. Unlike de Tracy, for whom the natural and social worlds were pellucid to the rational mind, the German romantics considered that human beings collectively and individually created their own reality in response to changing circumstances. For Hegel, who tried to give these ideas a systematic intellectual basis, the ideas of a particular age could not claim absolute validity in themselves for they were evidently relative to changing historical situations. If there *were* a rationality, a meaning, to history, it would have to be found in the whole process rather than in the partial aims of particular individuals and epochs. For the projects of individuals and epochs were the means by which the famous 'cunning of Reason' produced a result often far different from that intended by the original thinkers. These Hegelian ideas strongly influenced Marx, and it was Marxism, uniting both the French and the German trends, that put the concept of ideology in the forefront of political discourse. The young Marx, as a disciple of Hegel, sought to explain the changes in social and political ideas in terms of the social divisions occasioned by the different ways in which historically human beings had organized their productive labour. Later on, particularly with Engels, the positivistic tradition of de Tracy, the attempt at an objective science of society, was more prominent. At any rate, until the last few decades, the study of ideology, however conceived, was largely the preserve of those who related themselves in some way to the Marxist tradition.

However, the would-be objective scientific study of ideology in the manner of de Tracy has enjoyed a strong revival in the West after the Second World War, particularly in the United States. The catastrophe visited upon the world by the Nazi movement, the disillusionment of many as the excesses of Stalinism became known, and the perception of Soviet Communism as a monolithic threat to Western-style democracy prompted a concern to explain the origin and power of these ideas. And this concern was reinforced by the startling impact of Mao-tse Tung's 'thought' on Chinese society, particularly in the Great Leap Forward and the Cultural Revolution, as also by the evident power of ideals of national liberation in so many Third World countries. With these writers, the term 'ideology' took on a distinctly pejorative sense associated intellectually with irrationality and politically with the concept of totalitarianism. This antipathy was reinforced by the dominance of behaviourism in American political science and of analytical, linguistic philosophy in Britain, both of which had a strongly pragmatic, empirical approach aimed at debunking large-scale speculation by asking more mundane questions about what were regarded as matters of fact or of linguistic usage. On this view, the 'Age of Ideology' was past.[9] It belonged to the specific period of industrialization which, following the breakdown of traditional societies, had given rise to much intellectual ferment among rival groups. Nazism, and more particularly Communism, were nineteenth century hangovers with no relevance to advanced post-industrial societies, where technical problems with technical solutions were to the fore. Ironically, the term which Marx and his followers had done so much to popularize was now used as a weapon *against* Marxism. This 'end of ideology' approach, has obviously been severely challenged by the more troubled nature of the last three decades. The claim to objectivity has come increasingly under attack. The suspicion that a claim to an objective science of ideology may itself be ideological has gained ground. Feminists have cogently pointed out that our traditional ways of thinking about society are dominated by concepts that are very male-orientated[10]; the green movement has questioned the whole notion of technological progress[11]; the idea of the universal individual of the Enlightenment as a source of valid moral judgements has been put in doubt by those who see particular communities as the only plausible ground for moral agreement[12]; and, finally, the more radical forms of postmodernism reflect a society where ideas of truth, value and reality have been dissolved by a mixture of advertising, consumer choice and information technology.[13]

However varied the uses to which the term 'ideology' has been put over the last two centuries, two main lines have already been discerned. One is the French rationalist view of de Tracy and his colleagues from whom the term originated – though their optimistic rationalism was modified in the Anglo Saxon world with a heavy dose of empiricism. From its inception in the Enlightenment, through Durkheim to recent structuralist and empiricist revisions, it lays emphasis on the consensual nature of society and adopts a contemplative account of truth: truth is a correspondence with reality which observation and reason should enable all people of good will to recognize through the application, in the social sciences, of methods not radically different from those obtaining in the natural sciences. The second, and contrasting, line has Germanic roots, being originally associated with Hegel and Marx, and goes through Mannheim to Habermas. Here the emphasis is on the making of truth rather than on observation. Societies are seen rather as changing entities riven by conflict than held together by a stable consensus. Suspicious of any 'objective' way of deciding what is true, adherents of this view tend to adopt a coherence theory of truth. And this is particularly so in social questions to whose solution the methods of natural science are held to be alien. Of course, there is an infinite variety of positions between these two stark poles. To take but the most obvious example, both are fully represented within the Marxist tradition. It is to outlining the various ways in which these poles have been combined and distinguished that the following chapters are devoted.

2
Marx

Marx deserves a whole chapter to himself as it was the influence of his writings that gave the concept of ideology the wide currency that it now enjoys. Marx was familiar with the favourable view of ideology as a beneficial science of ideas in the works of de Tracy; but he preferred to give it the critical edge popularized by Napoleon's scorn of 'cloudy metaphysics'. It is the conservation of this critical edge and the different reasons for justifying it that gives to the Marxist tradition its interest. In Marx himself the pejorative sense of 'ideology' comprised two main elements: first, ideology was connected with idealism which, as a philosophical outlook, was unfavourably contrasted with materialism: any correct view of the world had to be, in some sense, a materialist view. Second, ideology was connected with the uneven distribution of resources and power in society: if the social and economic arrangements were suspect then so was the ideology that was a part of them.

It took Marx some time to work out an appropriate materialist theory of society and thus construct a framework for his concept of ideology; and it took him even longer to discuss how and why the social and economic foundation of society was essentially conflictual and the role that ideology played in this conflict. Indeed, as with so many of his central concepts, that of ideology is far from completely clear in Marx: his comments on ideology tend to be *obiter dicta* and he never produced a coherent account. Nevertheless, the main outlines are clear.

In his early writings, Marx established the background from which his treatment of ideology was to emerge. Initially he was interested in unmasking certain religious conceptions of the world and the high-flown conception of the state elaborated by his former master Hegel. In both these areas, two cognate processes were at work: first there was a movement from ideas to material reality instead of the other way round; and second, this inverted process not unnaturally obscured the real nature of things. Religion failed to realize that 'man makes religion, religion does not make man'. The idea of God, Marx claimed, following Feuerbach, is nothing but a projection of human aspirations. As long as God was conceived of as the creator of the world on whose designs humanity was dependent, then the true nature of human beings – to be in control of their own destiny, to be self-producing – would be frustrated. But it was not just that religion was idealist: it had its roots in a deficient reality which, at the same time, it helped to conceal. Therefore,

> the abolition of religion as the illusory happiness of the people is a demand for their real happiness. The demand to give up the illusions about their condition is a demand to give up a condition that requires illusion. The criticism of religion is therefore the germ of the criticism of the valley of tears whose halo is religion.[1]

This same dual process of idealist preconceptions and consequent concealment of reality was at work in Hegel's conception of the state. Since, according to Marx, Hegel started from the *idea* and regarded empirical reality as its manifestation, it was possible for Hegel to gloss over real and intractable conflicts in society by seeing them as ultimately parts of one harmonious ideal whole.

Thus Marx had set the scene for his conception of ideology. The mistaken conception of religion and politics that he criticized were not mere errors: these inverted conceptions had their basis in a real social world that was so misconstructed as to generate these compensatory illusions. So the next step was to investigate this social world, and the result of this investigation was what Marx called 'the materialist conception of history'. He elaborated this in a major work which criticized his idealist German contemporaries, and the prominent place allotted to ideology is indicated by the title – *The German Ideology*, the only work of Marx which contains his general ideas on society and history set out at length.

In *The German Ideology*, Marx sought to clarify the idea of inversion that he had got from his criticism of religion and of Hegel's political philosophy: it was a mistake to start from human consciousness and to proceed from this to an investigation of material reality. The correct approach was the other way round. The origin of the problem was not mistaken ideas but the misshapen nature of social reality which generated mistaken ideas: 'consciousness can never be anything else than conscious existence, and the existence of men is their actual life process. ... Life is not determined by consciousness but consciousness by life.'[2] The materialist conception of history held that it was the way in which human beings responded to their *material* needs that determined the rest of society. The basic social process was the satisfaction of the material needs for food, clothing and shelter. Human beings satisfied these material needs in the natural world that surrounded them, a world which they transformed for their own ends through the process of labour. It was this labouring process – which Marx sometimes called 'material practice' – that was the fundamental human activity, and it was the starting point for any valid social science. Marx summed this up as follows:

> The production of ideas, of conceptions, of consciousness, is at first directly interwoven with the material activity and the material intercourse of men, the language of real life. Conceiving, thinking, the mental intercourse of men, appear at this stage as the direct efflux of their material behaviour. The same applies to mental production as expressed in the language of politics, laws, morality, religion, metaphysics, etc., of a people. ... Men, developing their material production and their material intercourse, alter, along with this their actual world, also their thinking and the products of their thinking.[3]

Thus ideology had to be explained from material practice. But not all ideas were ideology and Marx did not wish simply to produce a more dynamic version of de Tracy's science of ideas. What made ideas into ideology was their connection with the conflictual nature of social and economic relationships which characterized the labour process. These conflicts were due, at bottom, to two factors. The first was the division of labour, beginning with the division between mental and manual labour, which implied the unequal distribution – both qualitatively and quantitatively – of both labour and its products. This entailed, second, the existence of private property and a situation in which the interest of the individual no longer coincided with that of the community. 'Out of this very contradiction', Marx continued:

> between the interest of the individual and that of the community the latter takes an independent form as the State, divorced from the real

interests of individual and community, and at the same time as an illusory communal life, always based, however, on the real ties.

The consequence of all this was that

all struggles within the State, the struggle between democracy, aristocracy, and monarchy, the struggle for the franchise, etc. etc. are merely the illusory forms in which the real struggles of the different classes are fought out among one another.[4]

It was their connection with this class struggle and its social and economic basis that gave certain ideas their ideological force. Society was in fact riven by conflicts of interest, but in order for it not to fall apart these oppositions were covered up by ideas which represented attempts to portray society as cohesive rather than conflictual by justifying the asymmetrical distribution of social and economic power. Hence Marx's famous statement that 'the ideas of the ruling class are in every epoch the ruling ideas',[5] since those who controlled economic production and distribution could also regulate the production and distribution of ideas. The example Marx chose to illustrate this was the period in Europe following the breakdown of the feudal system when the declining aristocracy and the growing bourgeoisie were struggling for mastery. Here power was, for a time, shared between monarchy, aristocracy and bourgeoisie and the doctrine of the separation of powers was elaborated by such as Locke and Montesquieu and proclaimed as an 'eternal law' of good government, though in reality it merely reflected the dispositions of the classes contending for power. What made ideas ideological, therefore, was that they concealed the real nature of social and economic relationships and thus served to justify the unequal distribution of social and economic resources in society. It followed that not all ideas were ideological but only those which served to conceal social contradictions. Hence, while all classes, including the working class, could produce ideology, it was only ideology in so far as it served to further the interest of the ruling class. And since society and its class structure was constantly changing, the same ideas could begin or cease to be ideological.

Although *The German Ideology* was Marx's most extended treatment of ideology, he did also mention it in his more mature works and some have claimed to see a crucial change of emphasis between the two. *The German Ideology* was written while Marx was still evolving his ideas and thus does not contain the specific analyses of capitalist society that Marx later produced. Its tone is polemical, it is unfinished and was never published by Marx. Moreover, certain of Marx's statements in *The German Ideology* have been thought too simplistic. The statement that 'if in all ideology men and their circumstances appear upside down as in a *camera obscura*, this phenomenon arises just as much from their historical life process as the inversion of objects on the retina does from their physical life process'[6] could give the impression that ideology was little more than an epiphenomenal illusion in which each idea was a distorted representation of some real 'thing'.[7] It is certainly true that Marx refines his concept of ideology in his later writings. In his earlier conceptions, as evidenced by his *camera obscura* reference, Marx thought of ideas as distorting or inverting reality because that reality was itself distorted or inverted. In his later writings, and particularly in *Capital*, Marx was keen to stress the distinction between the phenomenal forms of capitalist society and the essential relations of production that underlay them. In the famous passage on the 'Fetishism of Commodities', Marx writes:

> A commodity is a mysterious thing, simply because in it the social character of men's labour appears to them as an objective character stamped upon the product of that labour; because the relation of the producers to the sum total of their labour is presented to them as a social relation, existing not between themselves, but between the products of their labour. . . . It is a definite social relation between men which assumes, in their eyes, the form of a relation between things. In order to find an analogy, we must have recourse to the mist-enveloped regions of the religious world. In that world the productions of the human brain appear as independent beings endowed with life, and entering into relation both with one another and the human race. So it is in the world of commodities with the products of men's hands.[8]

Thus the social character of labour was concealed by the interchange of individual objects in a market which appeared thereby to be natural and unalterable. Ideology was here seen as deriving from the (real) surface relations of capitalist society which served to conceal the fundamental relations of production. Marx wrote:

> *everything appears reversed in competition*. The final pattern of economic relations as seen on the surface, in their real existence and consequently in the conceptions by which the bearers and agents of these relations seek to understand them, is very much different from,

and indeed quite the reverse of, their inner but concealed essential pattern and the conception corresponding to it.[9]

Here ideology still served, as in the earlier conception, to conceal and invert real relationships between people. But in addition Marx now concentrated on the way in which ideology was produced by the form in which people related together in the ordinary everyday transactions of capitalist society – in contrast to *The German Ideology* where he was considering the production of German intellectuals.[10] There was also less emphasis on illusion since ideology was seen here as reflecting something real, if decidedly partial, and also as being itself a real force. Marx's most striking example of this was the ideological power of concentrating simply on the labour market which was

> in fact a very Eden of the innate rights of man. There alone rule Freedom, Equality, Property and Bentham. Freedom, because both buyer and seller of a commodity, say of labour power, are constrained only by their own free will. They contract as free agents, and the agreement they come to is but the form in which they give legal expression to their common will. Equality, because each enters into relation with the other, as with a simple owner of commodities, and they exchange equivalent for equivalent. Property, because each disposes only of what is his own. And Bentham, because each looks only to himself.[11]

Here we have encapsulated Marx's account of ideology in capitalist society: the exploitation and inequality which were inherent in the relations of production were concealed by the appearance of free exchange in the sphere of circulation, concentration on which gave rise to the typically capitalist ideology of freedom, equality and so forth.

Before considering the difficulties in Marx's account, it may help to pose two questions which go to the heart of his ideas. First, in what sense, if any, does the working class have an ideology? Indeed, could Marx's own ideas constitute an ideology? Marx did occasionally give this impression by conflating the ideological nature of thought with the view that all thought was socially determined. In *The German Ideology*, for example, he said that

> Men are the producers of their conceptions, ideas, etc. – real, active men as they are conditioned by a definite development of their productive forces and of the intercourse corresponding to these, up

to its furthest forms. Consciousness can never be anything else than
conscious existence, and the existence of men is their actual
life-process.[12]

Although the general context might indicate that the sense of the
word 'ideology' was meant to be fairly specific, the most obvious
meaning is to equate ideology with consciousness in general. Again,
in the famous summary of the materialist conception of history in
the 1859 *Preface* to his *Critique of Political Economy*, Marx said that
in considering social and economic transformations of society

> a distinction should always be made between the material transform-
> ation of the economic conditions of production, which can be
> determined with the precision of natural science, and the legal,
> political, religious, aesthetic, or philosophic – in short, ideological
> forms in which men become conscious of this conflict and fight it
> out.[13]

Here again, the implication seems to be that all practical ideas,
including socialism, are ideological. It is true that there was no clear
distinction drawn by Marx between the social determination of
ideas and ideology in that he did not clearly indicate what kind of
social determination led to ideological thinking. Nevertheless, it is
equally clear that Marx would not have described his own ideas as
ideological: he described the aim of writing *The German Ideology* as
'to work out in common the opposition of our view to the
ideological view of German philosophy'.[14] Nor did he believe that
all socially-determined consciousness was ideological: even in the
passage quoted from the *Preface* he contrasts the study of 'the
material transformation of the economic conditions of production'
which 'can be determined with the precision of natural science' with
the 'ideological forms in which these become conscious of this
conflict and fight it out'.[15] Although this might mean that all
non-science was ideological, the pejorative sense of ideology, which
is by far the most common in Marx, must rule this out. Ideology, for
Marx, was not coterminous with the superstructure of ideas,
because the superstructure contained both ideological and non-
ideological elements; for example, in the *Theories of Surplus Value*
when discussing the relation of spiritual to material production,
Marx drew a distinction between the 'ideological component parts
of the ruling class' and the 'free spiritual production of this

particular social formation'.[16] An instance of this latter would be art and poetry to which capitalist production was hostile.

In general, then, for Marx, only those elements in the superstructure of ideas were ideological which served to perpetuate relations of denomination. It follows that any class can produce ideology, but, in so far as the working class generates ideology, it is bourgeois ideology; in so far as it is a genuinely socialist consciousness, it is not ideology being neither illusory nor confined to the surface appearance of bourgeois society.

The second question involves the common equation of Marx's concept of ideology with that of false consciousness.[17] The first point to be made is that Marx never used the expression 'false consciousness': the originator of this expression was Engels, whose rather jejune views on ideology will be discussed in the next chapter. Neither did Engels use it much, but the *locus classicus* is his letter to Mehring:

> Ideology is a process accomplished by the so-called thinker consciously, it is true, but with a false consciousness. The real motive forces impelling him remain unknown to him; otherwise it simply would not be an ideological process. Hence he imagines false or seeming motive forces. Because it is a process of thought he derives its form as well as its content from pure thought, either his own or that of his predecessors.[18]

Second, any attempt to equate ideology and false consciousness in Marx must rely heavily on *The German Ideology* as opposed to Marx's later writings on ideology as illusion as opposed to ideology as functional for everyday life. Third, it is evident that the notion of false consciousness is both too clear-cut and too general to encompass Marx's meaning. It is too clear-cut in that Marx does not operate with a true/false dichotomy; too vague because it is vital to know what kind of falsity is involved and, indeed, Marx's point is often that ideology is not a question of logical or empirical falsity but of the superficial or misleading way in which truth is asserted.[19]

Marx's conception of ideology contains several important difficulties. First, many of the main constituents of his concept are not clearly defined and thus leave room for ambiguity. For example, the debate surrounding the exact meaning of the *camera obscura* simile shows how unclear is Marx's attempt to explicate ideology by talking of inversion. For in order to solve the problem of ideology it is evidently necessary to do more than simply put things the right way up. Marx claimed to have found Hegel standing on his head and put him back on his feet – but what exactly *that* amounted to has given rise to as much disputation as anything else in Marx.

The ideas of reflection and echo in *The German Ideology* are too mechanically determinist and amount to little more than an inverted empiricism which continues the approach of de Tracy and the Enlightenment. In the same work, however, Marx claims that ideas are constitutive of the social world and not simply reflections of it.[20] The same ambiguity is true of the notion of contradiction which ideology is said to conceal and reproduce: the problem of how the concept of a contradiction, which is *prima facie* a logical concept, could apply to the real world is also extremely controversial.[21] First, this conceptual imprecision is partly due to the fact that Marx talked about ideology most extensively in *The German Ideology*, a work written while his thought was in rapid development and which was also left in untidy manuscript form which he would have wanted to revise considerably for publication. The other two places where ideology figures prominently – the *Preface* of 1859 and the beginning of *Capital* – are much briefer and written from different perspectives – not to say problematics. Thus Marx's treatment of ideology amount much more to 'a cluster of brilliant insights'[22] than to a fully worked out theory.

Second, Marx's concept of ideology is part of his general materialist conception of history which, again, is notoriously difficult to describe precisely. The socio-economic cannot be the only form of determination for the same socio-economic circumstances determine differently different things. How to privilege the socio-economic – and it must be privileged for the conception of history to be *materialist* – without lapsing into a crude reductionism is the major problem in Marxism. The traditional spatial metaphor employed by Marx of base and superstructure has been profoundly misleading and many later Marxists have been at pains to correct it – as we shall see in the next chapter.

Third, Marx's materialist conception of history and, inside it, his conception of ideology were conceived of as a critical tool to uncover the illusory conceptions of others. But how can he show that his own conceptions are not themselves ideological? Although Marx is not as open to this *tu quoque* as, say, Mannheim, it is evident that the distinction between science and ideology is not as neat as he does sometimes imply. He can claim to have avoided relativism by firmly adopting that standpoint of the proletariat, but it is at least arguable that this standpoint itself has proved illusory at several points. More potentially damaging, however, is the claim not that Marx was too proletarian but that he was too bourgeois. His optimistic rationalism, his strong emphasis on technology, his Eurocentrism are all the products of high Victorian capitalism, and it is to the ways in which twentieth century Marxists have sought to modify and refine many of his emphases that we now turn.

The Marxist Tradition

As the nineteenth century turned into the twentieth, Marx's ideas became systematized into the doctrine of a mass movement which meant that the evolution of the Marxist concept of ideology became subject to political factors. It should also be remembered that Marx's *The German Ideology*, where he dealt at great length with ideology, was not published until the mid-1920s. During this period there were three major developments in the Marxist treatment of ideology. First, in the Marxism of the Second International, the simplification of Marx's ideas into a general doctrine of economic determinism tended to bring the equation of ideology and false consciousness to the fore. Second – and in strong contrast with Lenin – the concept of ideology was stripped of its negative connotations and the idea of a socialist or Marxist ideology emerged. Third, with the failure of the revolutionary movement to develop adequately in the West, there was a growing impression that ideology might be a more powerful and independent force than had hitherto been imagined and consequently more attention and respect was paid to it among Western Marxists such as Gramsci and Althusser.

The systematization and vulgarization (in the best sense of the word) of Marx's theories was achieved above all by Engels. He alluded to ideology much more than did Marx (apart from *The German Ideology*), but in the context of general discussions of philosophy and history rather than as a foil for specific analyses. It is in his attempts to clarify the materialist conception of history that Engels most frequently mentions ideology. In a famous series of letters written in the late 1890s, he separated out economic, political and ideological relations and stated that, although the first two could affect the third, it was always the economic that determined them in the last instance:

> Men make their history themselves, only they do so in a given environment, which conditions it, and on the basis of actual relations already existing, among which the economic relations, however much they may be influenced by the other – the political and ideological relations – are still ultimately the decisive ones, forming the keynote which runs through them and alone leads to understanding.[1]

Taking over the base-superstructure metaphor from the Marx of 1859, Engels constructed a hierarchy of ideologies, citing religion and philosophy – in contrast to politics and law – 'as realms of ideology which soar still higher in the air',[2] Engels sometimes excluded politics and law from the ideological altogether and gave the impression that he considered ideologies to be more ideological the more removed they were from the material economic basis and the nearer they approached the top of the superstructure.

This connection of ideology with the ethereal was inspired by the influence on Engels of late nineteenth century rationalism and materialism and the straightforward methodological contrast with idealism. History, according to Engels, proceeded 'in the manner of a natural process and is subject to the same laws of motion'[3] and materialism began with recognizing this. Engels's main philosophical opponent, Dühring, was ideological in that he accepted an *a priori* method which 'consists in ascertaining the properties of an object by logical deduction from the concept of the object, instead of from the object itself'.[4] Dühring's ideas were 'pure ideology' which was 'deduction of reality not from itself but from a concept'.[5] On this view, ideology was an exclusive preoccupation with thoughts as opposed to reality:

> Every ideology, once it has arisen, develops in connection with the given concept material, and develops this material further; otherwise it would not be an ideology, that is, occupation with thoughts as with independent entities, developing independently and subject only to their own laws.[6]

Or again, in the passage already referred to, when Engels identified ideology with false consciousness, he described ideas as a process of thought in which the thinker derives its form as well as its content from pure thought, either his own or that of his predecessors. He works with mere thought material, which he accepts without examination as the product of thought, and does not investigate further for a more remote source independent of thought; indeed this is a matter of course to him, because, as all action is *mediated* by thought, it appears to him to be ultimately *based* upon thought.[7]

This view was founded on a kind of metaphysical materialism to which ideology was seen as the opposite. The falsity of ideology was not so much due to its origin or function as to its ontological status, its propensity to deal with things that simply were not there.

But there is also in Engels a strong connection between ideology and ignorance that reflects the influence of scientific rationalism. The false consciousness of the ideological thinker was so because 'the real motive forces impelling him remain unknown to him; otherwise it simply would not be an ideological process. Hence he imagines false or seeming motive forces.'[8] Engels's example here was taken from religion from what he called 'the erroneous, primitive conceptions of men about their own nature and external nature surrounding them'.[9] Engels's remarks on ideology obviously encountered the same difficulties as those of Marx. These were compounded in Engels by two further additions: first, the development of a rather jejune version of the materialist conception of history as an interaction of various factors in which ideology was neatly pigeonholed on the top of the superstructure, and second, the introduction of a materialist metaphysic in the shape of dialectical materialism which encouraged the narrow view of ideology as quite simply false. The effect of these two emphases was retrogressive when compared to Marx as they both neglect both the power and the subtlety of ideology.

Engels clearly retained a negative concept of ideology since he connected it with thought that was detached from reality and with ignorance. But he did sometimes talk generally of 'ideological superstructures'[10] as Marx did in 1859, and sometimes gave the impression that ideology was merely socially-determined thought. But the first person to declare roundly that Marxism was itself an ideology was Edward Bernstein whose attempts to revise Marx's ideas gained prominence around 1900. Bernstein based this conviction on the very revisionist idea that Marxism was based on a moral ideal and on the curious argument that Marxism must be an ideology because it consisted of ideas – and ideas were by definition ideological. Thus socialist conceptions of state and society were riddled with ideology. No political programme, including a socialist one, could do without 'a good dose of ideology'.[11]

If it was Bernstein's philosophically rather muddled revisions of Marxism that led him to describe it as ideological, the very opposite was the case with Lenin. For with him it was the sharpening of the class struggle that led him to ascribe an ideological position to every class – including the proletariat. Ideology thus lost its negative connotation: ideas were not deficient for their being ideological but solely from the class interest that they might serve. In the most famous passage expressing this idea, in his pamphlet *What is to be done?*, Lenin said:

> the *only* choice is – either bourgeois or socialist ideology. There is no middle course (for mankind has not created a 'third' ideology, and, moreover, in a society torn by class antagonisms there can never be a non-class or an above class-ideology). Hence, to belittle the socialist ideology *in any way, to turn aside from it in the slightest degree* means to strengthen bourgeois ideology.[12]

For Lenin these two very distinct forms of ideology were not the same as the consciousness of the classes concerned. Later in *What is to be done?* he stated that 'that history of all countries shows that the working class, exclusively by its own effort, is able to develop only trade-union consciousness'.[13] Therefore, socialist ideology had to be brought into the working class movement from the outside by a body of professional revolutionaries who had a superior grasp of political reality. The reason for this was that the workers, if left to themselves, would succumb to bourgeois ideology: 'The spontaneous development of the working-class movement leads to its subordination to bourgeois ideology . . . for the spontaneous working-class movement is trade-unionism, and trade-unionism means the ideological enslavement of the workers by the bourgeoisie.[14] An alternative ideology could only be generated by a socialist intelligentsia because bourgeois ideology was the ruling ideology: it has been around for so long that it appeared to be the natural way of looking at society and only the intervention of a vanguard party could point the workers in the right direction. Marxism was, moreover, a scientific ideology in that it corresponded to an objective reality. The success of the Bolsheviks in 1917 meant that Lenin's simplistic version of what ideology was became Marxist orthodoxy for generations and, in particular, his 'neutral' conception of ideology robbed it of any critical analytical power.

Lenin's view of ideology may have been simplistic but in the works of his Hungarian fellow-Communist Georg Lukacs it took on a much subtler form. First, it is clear that Lukacs's concept of ideology is as extensive as that of Lenin. It is true that, in certain passages, Lukacs seemed to equate ideology with false consciousness – as when he said that 'in the class struggles of the past the most varied ideologies, religions, moral and other forms of false consciousness were decisive'.[15] But this equation did not apply to all ideology, only to certain stages of it. What determined the validity of a view was not whether it was ideological or not, but the structural position of the class holding it: 'the bourgeoisie was quite unable to perfect its fundamental science, its own science of classes. . . . The barrier which converts the class consciousness of the bourgeoisie into "false" consciousness is objective: it is the class situation itself'.[16] And the superior class position of the proletariat did not make its views any less ideological – it just made them more scientific. Lukacs even talked of the degree of class consciousness of the proletariat being an indication of its ideological maturity. Historical materialism was, for him, an ideology, but not just an ideology: it was 'the ideological expression of the proletariat in its effort to liberate itself'.[17] Thus the validity of proletarian ideology lay in the future: it would be proved right in practice.

Where Lukacs did differ from Lenin was in his treatment of the difference between bourgeois and proletarian ideology. Previous to the arrival of the proletariat on the world stage, understanding the world had been blocked by the phenomenon for which Lukacs popularized the term 'reification'. Here Lukacs went explicitly to Marx's analysis of the fetishism of commodities in *Capital*, in which the social relations between persons became transformed – both subjectively and objectively – into relations between commodities. The world of things ruled human beings through objective laws that appeared to be independent of them; human beings thus became objects, passive spectators of a process that structured their lives for them. Starting from the economic division of labour, Lukacs traced the progress of this reification in the state and in modern bureaucracy – here borrowing from Max Weber's concept of 'rationality' inherent in industrial society.

According to Lukacs, the notion of reification was linked to that of totality. One of the results of reification was 'the destruction of every image of the whole'.[18] The specialization of labour and the general atomization of society meant that people and the world surrounding them were viewed as discrete, separate entities with no intrinsic connections. The bourgeoisie had necessarily to view things like this, for it was essential to their way of life to concentrate on some of the parts rather than the whole.

The central impetus of the reification process up until the present had been the all-pervasiveness of objectivity: in a reified world there were no subjects, no real choice. However, the oppressed, in order to free themselves, were forced to adopt the standpoint of the whole and question whether the parts were as objective and immovable as they seemed to be. Lukacs considered that the evolution of capital in society had not reached a point where the proletariat could destroy reification and become the subject and initiator of the historical process. Thus, while for Lenin the power of bourgeois ideology was due largely to its control of institutions for disseminating its views, for Lukacs the ideological subordination of the proletariat was more embedded in the very economic and social organization of capitalist society.

The difficulties of Lukacs's account of ideology are that it is excessively abstract and lacks almost any empirical reference. For the proletariat is not its own creator – it is created by the capitalist mode of production. And Lukacs had no theory of *how* the proletariat developed its own consciousness, except in the ultra-Left view that the Party alone was capable of representing the proletariat's 'ascribed' class consciousness. For the class consciousness of the proletariat that Lukacs talked so much about did not necessarily have any palpable existence. It was simply 'the thoughts and feelings appropriate to their objective situation'. 'This consciousness is, therefore'. Lukacs continued,

> neither the sum nor the average of what is thought or felt by the single individuals who make up the class. And yet the historically significant actions of the class as a whole are determined in the last resort by its consciousness and not by the thought of the individual – and these actions can be understood only be reference to this consciousness.[19]

Here Lukacs's idealist approach stands in stark contrast to the materialism of Engels. For whereas Engels attempted to give his concept of ideology a materialist basis by sometimes almost equating Marxism with natural science, Lukacs went in the opposite direction and posited a radical break between natural and social science and particularly gave an overwhelming role to ideology. From being a pale reflection of reality perched on the summit of the superstructure it became in Lukacs the driving force of history. But it was an account of ideology that was, in its way, just as removed from material reality as that of Engels.

With Antonio Gramsci the Marxist discussion of ideology reaches its high point. Gramsci took over the positive or neutral concept of ideology outlined by Lenin and Lukacs, but he devoted considerable space to discussing both the concept of ideology and also the details of its history and contemporary influence. There is another difference too: Lenin and Lukacs were writing at the time of the high tide of Marxist success; Gramsci's thinking about ideology was marked by the ebb of Marxism in Western Europe and the rise of Stalinism in Russia. There is, therefore, a less confident treatment, more of a resigned analysis, even a 'pessimism of the intellect', in Gramsci's famous phrase, however much this might be accompanied by optimism of the will. This tendency both to pay more attention to ideology and to treat it as more a matter of theoretical discussion than practical political activity is characteristic of Western Marxism as a whole.

Unlike Lenin and Lukacs, Gramsci did consider the negative concept of ideology, only to reject it. He did this on the grounds that the negative concept of ideology was too reductionist. He enumerated the steps leading to this error as follows:

(1) ideology is identified as distinct from the structure, and it is asserted that it is not ideology that changes the structures but vice versa;
(2) it is asserted that a given political solution is 'ideological'; i.e. that it is not sufficient to change the structure, although it thinks that it can do so; it is asserted that it is useless, stupid, etc.;
(3) one then passes to the assertion that every ideology is 'pure' appearance, useless, stupid, etc.[20]

The result of this process, evident in the work of Engels and Bukharin, was that 'the bad sense of the word has become widespread, with the result that the theoretical analysis of the concept of ideology has been modified and denatured'.[21] Gramsci therefore distinguished between organic ideologies and those which were arbitrary. An organic ideology was one which was necessary to a given historical structure – organic ideologies 'organise human masses, and create the terrain on which men move, acquire consciousness of their position, struggle, etc.'[22] Gramsci's paradigm for this broad sense of ideology was religion which he saw, like ideology, as producing 'a unity of faith between a conception of the world and a corresponding norm of conduct'.[23]

Although Gramsci pointed to the 'common sense' nature of ideology, he also laid stress on the role of intellectuals in almost *creating* ideology. Here Gramsci drew a distinction between 'traditional' and 'organic' intellectuals. Traditional intellectuals were intellectuals who, mistakenly, considered themselves to be autonomous of social classes and who appeared to embody a historical continuity above and beyond socio-political change. Examples would be writers, artists, philosophers and, especially, ecclesiastics. They were those intellectuals who survived the demise of the mode of production that gave them birth. The fact that they were linked to historically moribund classes, and yet pretended to a certain independence, involved the production of an ideology, usually of an idealist bent, to mask their real obsolescence. While the notion of a traditional intellectual was primarily a historical one, that of an organic intellectual was much more sociological. The extent to which an intellectual was organic was measured by the closeness of the connection of the organization of which he or she was a member to the class which that organization represented. Organic intellectuals articulated the collective consciousness or ideology of their class in the political, social and economic sphere.

Gramsci also drew a close connection between ideology and his concept of hegemony which he inherited from Lenin and Lukacs. Lukacs in particular had emphasized how the bourgeoisie obtained the consent of virtually the whole of society to its governance through so organizing the relations of production that its own dominance seemed natural. Gramsci took up this conception and integrated it with his emphasis on the role of intellectuals:

> The intellectuals of the historically progressive class, in the given conditions, exercise such a power of attraction that, in the last analysis, they end up by subjugating the intellectuals of the other social groups; they thereby create a system of solidarity between all

the intellectuals, with bonds of a psychological nature (vanity, etc.) and often of a cast character (technical-juridical, corporate, etc.).[24]

In other words, the world view of the ruling class was so thoroughly diffused by its intellectuals as to become the 'common sense' of the whole of society, the 'structure of feeling' in which it lived.[25] The bureaucratic and technological rationalism analysed by Weber was part of the capitalist ideological hegemony which functioned to repress any creative or innovatory initiatives of the working class. Gramsci considered this realization that for the most part the ruling class did not have to resort to force to maintain its dominance to be the core of his theory: 'it is even possible to affirm that present-day Marxism in its essential trait is precisely the historical-political concept of hegemony'.[26]

This conception of ideological hegemony was Gramsci's answer to the puzzle of how capitalism had been able to survive in the bourgeois democracies of the West. Moreover, while the bourgeoisie continued to exercise such a cultural hegemony, a proletarian revolution was impossible. To establish its own hegemony the working class must do more than struggle for its own narrow sectarian interests: it must be able to present itself as the representative of the interests of society as a whole. The establishment of a proletarian counter-hegemony was impossible without the active participation of the intellectuals of the working class. The Party was also an essential element here. Gramsci had a broader view of the Party than Lenin, since he conceived of it as deeply committed to an ideological and cultural struggle as well as to the seizure of state power. Gramsci was convinced that the Leninist strategy of neglecting the ideological hegemony of the bourgeoisie would not work in the advanced industrialized countries of the West. Thus he advocated a Party that was an educational institution offering a counter-culture whose aim was to gain an ascendancy in most aspects of civil society (as opposed to directly political institutions) before the direct attempt was made on state power. Unlike both Lenin and Lukacs, he was interested in ideology not just in its highly rationalized form as systematic political ideology, but also as religion, as 'common sense', and even as folklore. Thus his work forms a bridge between classical Marxism and the investigation of the connection between ideology and everyday life that will be discussed in Chapter 6. In particular, Gramsci broke down the strict

dichotomy between spontaneous consciousness and socialist ideology so prominent in the Bolshevik tradition and helped to
emphasize the complex pervasiveness of ideology in contemporary
society.

Finally, mention must be made of the contribution of the French
philosopher Louis Althusser to the Marxist concept of ideology.
This contribution combines two main ideas. The first is a strongly
determinist view of society which sees people simply as bearers of
social roles rather than as in any way autonomous subjects. The
second is a strict separation between ideology and science. In both
these ideas. Althusser, as an anti-humanist and an anti-historicist,
differed sharply from Lukacs.

Like Gramsci, Althusser is against any conception of ideology as
false consciousness. This is partly because he is not interested
primarily in the possible falsehood of ideology but rather with the
function it performs; more importantly he does not see ideology as a
product of people's minds but as having itself a quasi-material
existence which defines what people think and is embodied in our
society in what he calls 'ideological state apparatuses' such as
churches, trade unions and schools. He expresses this idea as
follows:

> In ideology men do indeed express, not the relation between
> themselves and their conditions of existence, but *the way* they live the
> relation between them and their conditions of existence. This
> presupposes both a real relation and an '*imaginary*', lived relation.[27]

Thus ideology is not merely an illusory representation of reality: it is
the means through which people live their relation to reality. As an
example, Althusser cites the fact that

> In the ideology of *freedom*, the bourgeoisie lives in a direct fashion its
> relation to its conditions of existence: that is to say, its real relation
> (the law of the liberal capitalist economy), *but incorporated* in an
> imaginary relation (all men are free, including free workers). Its
> ideology consists in this word-play about freedom, which betrays just
> as much the bourgeois will to mystify those it exploits (free!) in order
> to keep them in harness, by bondage to freedom, as the need of the
> bourgeoisie to *live* its class domination as the freedom of the
> exploited.[28]

Thus it is a characteristic feature of ideology that it persuades
people of their freedom and autonomy: 'all ideology has the

function (which defines it) of "constituting" concrete individuals as subjects'.[29] The word 'subject' is taken here both in the sense of an independent person and also in the other sense of 'a subjective being, who submits to a higher authority, and is therefore stripped of all freedom except that of freely accepting his submission'.[30] On this pessimistic view, ideology inescapably makes us into prisoners of ourselves.

Althusser also believes that ideology (of some sort) is a permanent feature of society. He is strongly influenced by Freud here and declares that 'ideology is eternal, exactly like the unconscious'.[31] Ideology is a social cement and thus in contemporary capitalist society it cements a system of class domination. Nevertheless,

Human societies secrete ideology as the very element and atmosphere indispensable to their historical respiration and life. Only an ideological world outlook could have imagined societies without ideology and accepted the utopian idea of a world in which ideology (not just one of its historical forms) would disappear. . . . Historical materialism cannot conceive that even a communist society could ever do without ideology.[32]

For even a communist society will need cementing.

The second main feature of Althusser's conception of ideology is more easily described. It is the sharp contrast he makes between ideology and science. By criticizing ideology, science poses the problem in an entirely different manner and therefore arrives at a different sort of solution. Epistemology is radically separate from sociology: the truth of scientific theory is not dependent on history as the methods and validation of theory, like those of mathematics, are internal and peculiar to it. The main science Althusser has in mind is, Marxism, though he is willing to admit psychoanalysis also into this category. Unfortunately he does not tell us how to judge whether or not a theory *is* scientific – many having considered both Marxism and psychoanalysis to be prime examples of *un*scientific thought.

A lot of Althusser's writing is obscure and ambiguous. It does, however, have the advantage of linking ideology to an institutional context and to the practices of everyday life. But the strict opposition of ideology to science is a mere assertion on his part and is inspired more by Lenin's opposition of trade union consciousness to the science available through the Party than by any argument.

Most importantly, the excessive structural determinism of his theory leaves no room for autonomous action by people and in particular their reflexive understanding of the structure in which they are embedded and the possibility of their doing something about it.[33] With the work of Althusser and Gramsci, building on some of Marx's own ideas, the Marxist concept of ideology has begun to incorporate some of the non-Marxist approaches to which we now turn.

The Non-Marxist Tradition

The attention devoted to Marxist conceptions of ideology is justified in that, until comparatively recently, discussions of ideology were not prominent in non-Marxist social and political thought. Nevertheless, parallel to the Marxist thinkers discussed in the last chapter, there were important developments in the social sciences in general which influenced the understanding of ideology. For example, the two thinkers who (with Marx) were the founding fathers of sociology – Weber and Durkheim – produced discussions about the genesis and validity of ideas which contributed substantially to subsequent treatments of ideology – Weber as the inspirer of much later empirical investigation in the Anglo-Saxon world and Durkheim as the forerunner of structuralist analyses. The turn of the century also saw the beginnings of psychoanalysis which has had its own rather pessimistic contribution to make to the discussion. Finally, we shall return to the German historicist tradition in the person of Karl Mannheim who produced a comprehensive theory of ideology that is still a reference point for today's discussions.

Weber very rarely mentioned the word 'ideology'. As we saw in the previous chapter, his discussions of the 'iron cage' of increasing bureaucracy and rationalization had a profound effect even on such a very different thinker as Lukacs. But his long, and heavily qualified, search for objectivity in politics places him uncertainly in the democratic tradition moving from Destutt de Tracy to much current Anglo-Saxon political science. Weber was well aware that the undermining potential of the Marxist concept of ideology could be turned against the Marxists themselves – a point later to be elaborated in full by Mannheim. 'The materialist conception of history', he wrote, 'is not to be compared to a cab that one can enter or alight from at will, for once they enter it, even the revolutionaries themselves are not free to leave it.'[1] Indeed, Weber went as far as to reject the idea of an 'absolutely "objective" scientific analysis of "social phenomena" independent of special and "one-sided" viewpoints according to which – expressly or tacitly, consciously or unconsciously – they are selected, analysed and organised for expository purposes'.[2] Nevertheless, he believed that a value-free social science was at least a legitimate aim. Whatever the particular values and prejudices of thinkers, their conclusions should be valid in terms which were in principle accessible to everyone – even, as he unfortunately put it, to a Chinaman. It is this aspect of Weber's thought that has been one-sidely taken up and so stridently pursued by many American studies of ideology in the post-war decades.

If Weber sometimes sounds ambivalent about his approach of ideology, Durkheim is much more firmly anchored in the tradition of Bacon and the *ideologues*. In *The Rules of Sociological Method*, ideology was firmly opposed to science. The 'ideological method' consisted in 'the use of notions to govern the collation of facts rather than deriving notions from them'.[3] Science, on the other hand, consisted in the study of social facts which 'constitute a fixed object, a constant standard which is always to hand for the observer, and which leaves no room for subjective impressions or personal observations'.[4] Durkheim was not interested in the social origins of some preconceptions, but viewed them – like Bacon, to whom he makes explicit reference – as innate bents of the human mind. It is true that in the most famous of the works of his maturity, *The Elementary Forms of the Religious Life*, Durkheim located the source of religion in the social structure and perceived it as a factor of social integration. He saw the forms of religion and the form of society as being, in some sense, identical. Although Durkheim did not use the word 'ideology' to describe religion here, it seems applicable and, at first sight at least, incompatible with his earlier Baconian analysis of ideology. But presumably Durkheim would have said that he was considering religion as a social fact and his sociology was devoted to demolishing false ideas about religion by establishing its social function as society's collective representation of itself. In any case with his strong emphasis on objective structure and the rejection of the subjectivity of the German historical tradition, Durkheim laid the foundation for much of the later sociological discussion of ideology in the post-war world.

Neither Weber nor Durkheim could be described as having the confidence in reason that characterized Marx; but at least they were fairly optimistic about the possibility of improving society and thus qualified as progressive thinkers. But the end of the nineteenth century also witnessed currents of thought that profoundly mistrusted the power of reason and gave pride of place to the irrational in accounting for human beliefs and actions. This view tended to have strong conservative implications. Its most prominent representatives – whose influence is as strong today as ever – were Sigmund Freud and Vilfredo Pareto.

As is well known, Freud's main ideas were not immediately connected with the study of ideology. Psychoanalysis investigated the individual psyche. It was above all in the individual mind that Freud located the notions of repression – whereby the ego relegated unacceptable instinctual impulses to the realm of the unconscious – and of rationalization whereby the true causes of obsessional neuroses were concealed by an account of secondary motives. Nevertheless, the ideas of Freud do have social and political implications and indeed, when considering these implications, he worked on the assumption that 'we base everything on the psyche of the mass in which psychic processes occur as in the psychic life of the individual'.[5] Indeed it is striking how much Althusser, with his notion of ideology as largely unconscious of its own preconditions, takes from Freud. For Freud believed that the basic factor in politics was the erotic relationship of the group to the leader and that the function of ideology was to reinforce libidinal ties between rulers and ruled which would result in a positive attitude towards authority. In looking at artificial groups such as churches and armies, Freud claimed that groups capable of subsisting had to have 'many equals, who can identify themselves with one another, and a single person superior to them all'.[6] In consequence, Freud modified the widespread description of human beings as 'herd animals' and asserted that man was 'a horde animal, an individual creature in a horde led by a chief'.[7] This view was most clearly worked out in *Totem and Taboo* where Freud firmly placed the question of the origin and maintenance of political power in the context of the Oedipus complex and described the continued acceptance of political authority to feelings of guilt. Positing some kind of initial rebellion of sons against their father, Freud continued:

> The situation created by the removal of the father contained an element which in the course of time must have brought about an extraordinary increase of longing for the father. Thus the bitter feelings against the father which had incited to the deed could subside in the course of time, while the longing for him grew and an ideal could arise having as a content the fullness of power and the freedom from restriction of the conquered primal father as well as the willingness to subject themselves to him.[8]

Thus every revolution ended in restoration and all political arrangements were counter-revolutionary responses to the archetypal origin rebellion.

In Freud's later and more rationalistic work, *The Future of an Illusion*, the problem of ideology received a wider treatment. Here the attachment of the led to their leaders was viewed as to some extent the product of a defence mechanism whereby human beings protect themselves against an object which causes fear by identifying themselves with it and assuming some of its features. Like Durkheim, Freud was interested in examining primitive society and the origin of religion in order to understand ideology. At times he talks as though culture, and particularly religion, involved a repressive element necessary for the maintenance of any civilization. But at the same time, again like Durkheim, he put faith in the ability of scientific investigations to bring about a more rational society. Nevertheless, the impact of Freud's work has undoubtedly been conservative: his Hobbesian view of human nature, and his undermining of the concept of reason, have generally yielded pessimistic social and political conclusions which have been widely used in the United States to discredit radicalism.[9] But psychoanalysis can be turned to radical, as well as conservative, ends, as is shown by Freud's maverick disciple Wilhelm Reich.

It was the rise of Fascism that Reich was particularly concerned to explain with the help of psychoanalytical categories. Fascist ideology, according to Reich, arose from sadistic impulses that were given a political rationalization in times of crises. These sadistic impulses were the result of age-old sexual repression, particularly in the authoritarian family which was 'the factory in which the state's structure and ideology are moulded'.[10] He continued:

> When sexuality is prevented from attaining natural gratification, owing to the process of sexual repression, what happens is that it seeks various kinds of substitute gratifications. Thus, for instance, natural aggression is distorted into brutal sadism, which constitutes as essential part of the mass-psychological basis of those imperialistic wars that are instigated by a few.[11]

Unlike Freud, Reich's conclusion was libertarian and socialist; removal of repression, particularly in the sexual field, was the necessary precondition for all emancipation.

The psychological approach of Freud was given a more general form by Vilfredo Pareto. In Pareto's view, the part played in social phenomena by un-logical behaviour was overwhelming. He was more sceptical than Freud and held that any belief in reason, truth or progress was to be classed as non-logical. Basic to human activity were what Pareto called 'residues' – feelings which correspond to certain human instincts. In the social and political sphere, these 'residues' gave rise to 'derivations' which were would-be coherent sets of beliefs that directed people's actions. Pareto was not concerned to establish the falsity of these 'derivations', only the fact that they are not accepted on any rational grounds. But since Pareto also believed that all societies were inevitably governed by élites which replaced each other, he held that the role of derivations was to promote or undermine the established order in the interests of one or other élite. The content of the derivation was illusory in that it tended to promise the unattainable. Pareto's extremely prolix works exemplify the ultimate in conservative pessimism. They contain the positivist approach of Bacon and de Tracy shorn of its rationalist element. For Pareto's sceptical views allow no room for such ideas as truth, reason or progress which are, and always will be, illogical components of ideologies manipulated by élites in their own interests. It is a relief to turn from Pareto to Mannheim whose work represented the high point of the German historicist tradition aiming to assimilate the insights of both Marx and Weber.

If it was Marx and his followers who established the problem of ideology as an inescapable part of social-political discussion, it was Karl Mannheim who, in the words of the author of a magisterial work on the topic, 'produced the first and so far the last comprehensive elaboration of a theory of ideology'.[12] This theory was put forward in Mannheim's book *Ideology and Utopia* first published in 1929 in the midst of the political and social turmoil that was tearing apart the Weimar Republic. Mannheim's intention was to extend the insights of Marx and others so as to produce a comprehensive theory of ideology. This theory, or 'sociology of knowledge' as he came to call it, would uncover the historically limited and thus partial nature of all political viewpoints and so provide the groundwork for a more harmonious, integrative and progressive interpretation of the discordant politics of his time. It would provide a research programme to counter the corrosion of values produced by the spread of industrial capitalism.

As befitted a pupil of Lukacs, Mannheim was against any straightforward science of ideas based on unchanging concepts of reason and nature. He wrote:

> What we have to show, as against Enlightenment, is that the most general definitions and categories of Reason vary and undergo a process of alteration of meaning – along with every other concept – in the course of intellectual history. It is rather questionable in general whether 'form' can be sharply separated from 'content'. We always ask to what extent the particular content which, after all, is unqualifiedly historical, determines the particular formal structure. If however, one tries to evade the problems involved in historicity by assuming a timeless 'form as such', 'concept as such', 'value as such', and similar 'as such' structures, then it becomes impossible to say anything concrete in methodology at all.[13]

In his insistence that thought and expression were firmly embedded in history, Mannheim was much influenced by two late nineteenth century German theorists. Wilhelm Windelband had rejected the idea of a unity of the sciences and insisted that the natural and the human sciences had two radically different aims: the natural sciences searched for general and universal laws into which individual phenomena could be fitted; the historical sciences were concerned with the description of historical and cultural phenomena that were unique. Wilhelm Dilthey expressed this distinctiveness of the human sciences slightly differently; for him, they involved a reflective understanding of the meaning of cultural phenomena which placed a strong emphasis on the subjectivity of both the observer and the observed. This view – that all thought is historically conditioned – is sometimes known as 'historism'. This whole problem of how we can uncover the meanings of past events or writings (or even present ones springing from a different culture) is obviously both wide-ranging and crucial. The questions of how interpretation, understanding and explanation are possible between different epochs and cultures, whether they can be brought to some common denominator, whether the methods of the natural sciences (themselves viewed as problematic) can be applied to the human sciences, first formulated clearly in the late nineteenth century, have given rise to controversies that continue unabated today.

Although he was strongly influenced by the anti-positivist tendencies of Dilthey and others, Mannheim tried to avoid lapsing into relativism. Nevertheless, his treatment of ideology, leans heavily in the direction of his German 'historist' predecessors. This is very clear in his approach to Marxism which is his point of departure in developing his own self-reflective theory of ideology. Previous to Marx, there existed only a 'particular' conception of ideology. Mannheim traced the origin of this conception from Bacon and Machiavelli to the rational and calculating approach of the Enlightenment. This 'particular' conception 'will always strive in accordance with the psychology of interests to cast doubt upon the integrity of the adversary and to deprecate his motives' by pointing out the personal and psychological roots of intellectual bias. The particular conception of ideology merely rejected *what* was said and convicted its opponent of error – the very condition of which was a shared conceptual framework; with the 'total' conception of ideology, by contrast, it was the conceptual framework itself which was brought into question:

> When we attribute to one historical epoch one intellectual world and to ourselves another one, or if a certain historically determined social stratum thinks in categories other than our own, we refer not to the isolated cases of thought-content, but to fundamentally divergent thought-systems and to widely differing modes of experience and interpretation. We touch upon the theoretical or noological level whenever we consider not merely the content but also the form, and event the conceptual framework of a mode of thought as a function of the life-situation of a thinker.[14]

It was Marxist theory, Mannheim says quite justly, which 'first achieved a fusion of the particular and total conceptions of ideology'.[15] But Marxist positions could be formed against Marxism itself:

> As long as someone does not call his own position into question but regards it as absolute, while interpreting his opponents' ideas as a mere function of the social positions they occupy, the decisive step forward has not yet been taken. . . . In contrast to this special formulation, the general form of the total conception of ideology is being used by the analyst when he has the courage of subjecting not just the adversary's point of view but all points of view, including his own, to the ideological analysis.[16]

Mannheim's conclusion from the above was that with 'the emergence of the general form of the total conception of ideology, the simple theory of ideology develops into the sociology of knowledge. What was once the intellectual armament of a party is transferred into a *method of research* in social and intellectual history generally.'[17] This sociology of knowledge established a framework in which to investigate the relationship between changing structures of thought and changing historical situations. This raises two preliminary questions. First, what sort of knowledge does the sociology of knowledge investigate? It is not the knowledge of discrete facts of mathematical propositions, but rather 'the attempt to reconstruct the whole outlook of a social group, and neither the concrete individuals nor the abstract sum of them can legitimately be considered as bearers of this ideological thought-system as a whole.'[18] In other words, these 'ideological thought-systems' are rather like Weber's ideal types which are than imputed to social groups – though Mannheim did not always escape the danger of circularly defining the groups in terms of the imputed ideas. Second, what is the relationship of these thought systems to society? Mannheim did not define precisely the nature of this relationship which he referred to as the 'existential determination of knowledge'. He insisted that it was not a straightforward causal relationship, nor did he wish to reduce knowledge to its social origins.[19] The main point in investigating the connections between ideas and social structure was that this was at least a necessary condition for the very understanding of such ideas: those ignorant of social context would not know what they were talking about.

Mannheim was at pains not to be guilty of the 'genetic fallacy' – the deduction of the validity of an idea directly from its origins.

Indeed, he insisted that, in the first instance at least, his total theory of ideology was non-evaluative. This was in contradistinction to the 'special' theory of Marxism which, in his view, saw only its opponents' thought as ideological without subjecting itself to the same critique. Mannheim's aim was, initially, to conduct 'a purely empirical investigation through description and structural analysis of the ways in which social relationships, in fact, influence thought'.[20] This in turn could lead to the question of how far this interrelationship affected the validity of thought. But he pointed out that 'it is important to notice that these two types of enquiry are not necessarily connected and one can accept the empirical results without accepting the epistemological conclusions'.[21] Indeed, he went as far as to insist that 'the fact that our thinking is determined by our social position . . . is often the path to political insight'.[22]

A major difficulty in grasping what Mannheim was saying is that he used the word 'ideology' in different senses according as to whether his interests were primarily historical or methodological. In the historical sections of *Ideology and Utopia*, for example, he described ideologies as 'the situationally transcendent ideas which never succeed *de facto* in the realization of their project contents'[23] and thus do not in the end disturb the existence of current social and political arrangements. These ideologies were incongruent with their period, either because they prevented human beings from adapting to the needs of the period, or because they cloaked other interests by reference to myths and ideals, or because they misdescribed social relations in terms of superseded historical categories.[24] They were, in other words, rather like the products of Gramsci's traditional intellectuals. Utopian ideas, by contrast, 'are not ideologies in the measure and in so far as they succeed through counteractivity in transforming the existing historical reality into one more in accord with their own conceptions'.[25] Since utopian ideas were 'only those orientations transcending reality which, when they pass over into conduct, tend to shatter, either partially or wholly, the order of things prevailing at the time',[26] the distinction between ideologies and utopias can only be clearly established after the event. But when he was dealing with broader questions of method, Mannheim adopted a wider definition of ideology. Indeed, when he talked of the sociology of knowledge, he preferred to substitute the term 'perspective' in order to avoid the pejorative moral connotation of 'ideology'.[27]

The central question raised by Mannheim's general total conception of ideology is whether it leads to a hopeless relativism. For he himself was careful to point out that his own conceptions were in no especially privileged position: 'The general form of the total conception of ideology is being used by the analyst when he has the courage to subject not just the adversary's point of view but all points of view, including his own, to the ideological analysis.'[28] But Mannheim refused the choice between an objectivity based on timeless principles unmediated by historical change and a relativism that would abandon any search for truth. Nor did he choose a middle path between them, for he rejected the presuppositions of both views, insisting that his own approach 'becomes relativism only when it is linked with the other static ideal of eternal, unperspectivist truths independent of the subjectivist experiences of the observer, and when it is judged by this alien ideal of absolute truth'.[29] While not wishing to deny that there was 'an irrevocable residue of evaluation inherent in the structures of all thought', Mannheim claimed a distinction between 'relationism' (as he described his own view) and relativism:

> relationism does not signify that there are no criteria of rightness and wrongness in a discussion. It does insist, however, that it lies in the nature of certain assertions that they cannot be formulated absolutely, but only in terms of the perspective of a given situation.[30]

This relationist approach did not treat all perspectives as equal, for

> as in the case of visual perspective, where certain positions have the advantage of revealing the decisive features of the object, so here pre-eminence is given to that perspective which gives evidence of the greatest comprehensiveness and the greatest fruitfulness in dealing with empirical materials.[31]

The result of such investigations would be some sort of synthesis, but one which was neither simply additive nor capable of laying claim to any absolute status. Mannheim may have been optimistic about the possibility of achieving even such a limited synthesis and also suitably vague as to the criteria of success, but the charge of relativism is clearly misplaced.

In the task of advancing social knowledge, Mannheim attached a privileged role to intellectuals. Any progressive perspective would have to 'retain and utilize much of the accumulated cultural acquisitions and social energies of the previous epoch'.[32] He continued: 'such an experimental outlook, increasingly sensitive to the dynamic nature of society and to its wholeness is not likely to be developed by a class occupying a middle position but only by a relatively classless stratum which is not too firmly situated in the social order'.[33] He insisted that the class and status ties of such a 'socially unattached intelligentsia' did not simply disappear. On the contrary, it was precisely the social position of intellectuals that gave them their several advantages. First, they had benefited from an educational system which replicated the conflicting tendencies of society at large: most other citizens were confined to a particular sector of society through being embedded in the social process of production. Second, they tended to be recruited from several classes and thus already possessed at least the raw material for a dynamic and flexible approach. Third, a large part of their activity was directed towards the study of other periods and places and thus had to possess the skills of 'interpretative understanding' necessary for moving towards a total perspective. In summary, Mannheim said that

> we owe the possibility of mutual interpretation and understanding of existent currents of thought to the presence of such a relatively unattached middle stratum which is open to the constant influx of individuals from the most diverse social classes and groups with all possible points of view. Only under such conditions can the incessantly fresh and broadening synthesis, to which we have referred, arise.[34]

Mannheim's views on the potential role of intellectuals are open to several objections. It has been maintained, for instance, that intellectuals are not as free-floating as he suggested in that they have been largely incorporated into institutions themselves patterned on the needs of society.[35] Although it is remarkable how many prominent intellectuals from Aristotle to Marx, and Mannheim himself, had cosmopolitan backgrounds,[36] this tendency does seem to be on the wane, due to the increasing organization and bureaucratization of society in the twentieth century. Again, Mannheim seems over-optimistic about the ease with which those tied to partial insights might be persuaded to adopt a larger

perspective. But there are certain common charges against Mannheim which are clearly misplaced.

He is not particularly élitist, reserving a suitably modest role for
intellectuals in the tentative promotion of a progressive synthesis:
Mannheim himself is more inclined to think that those who lay claim
to absolute and unchallengeable forms of knowledge (or even
unchallengeable methods of acquiring it) are most liable to emerge
as an élite. But the central objection to Mannheim's treatment of
the intellectual is that it is self-refuting. In a widely-used book,
Robert Merton wrote: 'Mannheim's conception of the general total
ideology . . . leads at once, it would seem, to radical relativism with
its familiar vicious circle in which the very propositions asserting
such relativism are *ipso facto* invalid.'[37] But this so-called 'Mannheim paradox' is by no means so clear-cut and comparisons of
Mannheim with Baron Munchausen trying to extricate himself from
the bog by pulling on his own pigtail are wide of the mark. For
Mannheim was not saying that intellectuals escape social determination – nor did he identify social determination with falsehood. On
the contrary, it was the very social position of the intellectuals which
enabled them to achieve a broader perspective. 'New forms of
knowledge', he claimed, 'in the last analysis, grow out of the
conditions of collective life and do not depend for their emergence
upon the prior demonstration by a theory of knowledge that they
are possible; they do not need to be first legitimized by an
epistemology.'[38] Whether intellectuals are in fact capable of the
task Mannheim assigns to them is an empirical not a logical
question.

An eminent professor has characterized Mannheim as 'an
inferior thinker, if ever there was one'.[39] It is true that his thought is
both vague and ambiguous in crucial areas – particularly when he
uses ideology both in the broad sense of thought subject to social
determination that renders it partial, and in the more restricted,
negative sense of self-interested illusions perpetuated by social
groups, and his over-broad sense of ideology tends to rob it of its
critical edge. But, although Mannheim's writings often do lack
precision, it is more accurate (as well as more generous) to see
Mannheim as the thinker who, as far as ideology is concerned,
'remains the first and most prominent scholar to have touched on
almost every aspect of the arguments mustered by contemporary
writers'.[40] The rather bleak passages at the end of *Ideology and*

Utopia foreshadow the debate on the 'end of ideology' in the United States and his 'total' theory of ideology plays the same role with regard to discussions of interpretation, meaning and communication that are to be found in such current theories as those of Habermas. These points will be elaborated in the next two chapters.

Ideology in
the United States

In spite of Mannheim's attempts to demonstrate the all-pervasiveness of ideological thinking, the positivist tradition of a restrictive definition of ideology and a discussion of it that claimed not itself to be ideological has been alive and well since the Second World War and living mainly in America. The comparatively recent growth of interest in ideology here is impressive; the prestigious *Encyclopaedia of the Social Sciences* (1930–35) contains no reference to ideology, whereas its successor of 1968, the *International Encyclopaedia of the Social Sciences*, has two lengthy articles on the subject.[1] Much of this positivist discussion of ideology harks back to Napoleon's dismissal of it as irrational and dangerously opposed to the pursuit of material interests.[2] This view reflected the predominance of behaviouralism in post-war American political science and the stress on ordinary language and linguistic analysis in British philosophy. The horrors of Nazism were fresh in many minds. Disillusion with Soviet Russia was also a factor making for an equation of ideology with extremism and the confidence that a value-free social science could establish some sort of adequate pragmatic approach to social improvement. An example of this attitude is to be found in the 'end of ideology' debate. Although many of the contributors to this debate were excellent examples of Mannheim's description of contemporary social scientists as 'talking past each other', they do bring into focus the approach to ideology still strong in Anglo-Saxon political science.

In one sense, Mannheim himself can be seen as a precursor of the 'end of ideology' thesis – or more appropriately, in his own terms, an 'end of utopia' thesis. In the final pages of *Ideology and Utopia*, he posed the pessimistic question:

> Must not the gradual reduction of politics to economics towards which there is at least a discernible tendency, the conscious rejection of the past and of the notion of historical time, the conscious pushing aside of every 'cultural ideal', be interpreted as a disappearance of every form of Utopianism from the political arena as well?[3]

While admitting the possibility that life in a world devoid of any transcendent element either in utopian or in ideological form was 'perhaps the only form of actual existence that is possible in a world which is no longer in the making', he nevertheless suggests that

> whereas the decline of ideology represents a crisis only for certain strata, and the objectivity which comes from the unmasking of ideologies always takes the form of self-clarification for society as a whole, the complete disappearance of the utopian element from human thought and action would mean that human nature and human development would take on a totally new character. The disappearance of utopia brings about a static state of affairs in which man himself becomes no more than a thing.[4]

One of the first post-war writers to give the idea of the end of ideology prominence ended his polemic against Marxism, entitled *Opium of the Intellectuals* (1955), with a conclusion headed 'End of Ideology?'. In spite of the question mark, Raymond Aron's view was quite clear:

> by different routes, either spontaneously or with the help of the police, the two great societies of our time have come to suppress the conditions of ideological debate, have integrated the workers, and imposed a unanimous adherence to the principles of the regime. The debate remains a burning one in those countries of the second rank who are not entirely at home in the ideological camp to which they belong; too proud to accept their *de facto* dependence, too arrogant to admit the dissidence of the internal proletariat reflects a national failure rather than a decree of history, fascinated by the power which spreads terror, prisoners of the geography which tolerates criticism and abuse but which forbids escape.[5]

Seymour Martin Lipset also ended his influential book *Political Man* with a chapter entitled 'The End of Ideology' (no question mark this time) which came to the same firm conclusion: since the fundamental problems of the industrial revolution had been solved, 'the democratic class struggle will continue, but it will be a fight without ideologies'.[6] This theme was given its most consistent elaboration by Daniel Bell, who in his book *The End of Ideology* (again!) declared that 'ideology, which was once a road to action, has become a dead end'.[7] Bell directly compared ideology to religion: ideology was religion's successor, appealing to the same sort of faith, passion and irrationality. But, unlike Gramsci who also drew strong parallels between religion and ideology, Bell drew the definitional boundaries of both very tightly, and his approach depends heavily for its validity on an equivocation between the decline of ideology and the decline of the 'old ideologies' – principally Nazism and Soviet Communism.[8]

Although much of the debate over the end of ideology thesis is semantic, the plausibility of the thesis does involve some substantive assumptions. Although the conclusions of the above authors can be debated even on their own terms, the point here is the more general one that the attempt to restrict the concept of ideology and even to eliminate it from Western society (and thereby by implication from the writings of the proponents of the thesis) has definite – and questionable – premises. The two most obvious of these premises are, first, the linkage made at the time by several prominent political theorists of the immediate post-war era between ideology and totalitarianism; and second, the attempt by sociologists to contrast ideology with science.

As to the first, Michael Oakshott's very influential essay *Rationalism in Politics* exalted practical, traditional knowledge, which could not be formulated in propositions and was only to be acquired in practice, with technical knowledge that was preoccupied with clearly formulated statements and a self-enclosed certainty whose main principle was rationalism. And rationalist politics were responsible for the advance of ideology in that they were 'the politics of the felt need, the felt need not qualified by a genuine, concrete knowledge of the permanent interests and direction of movement of a society, but interpreted by "reason" and satisfied according to the technique of an ideology: they are the politics of the book'.[9] In Oakshott's disciple Greenleaf this practical, traditional knowledge was to be found in Conservatism which, being a disposition, could not be ideological. In Minogue's even more extremely partial view, 'ideologies can be specified in terms of a shared hostility to modernity: to liberalism in politics, individualism in practice, and the market in economics', and therefore 'ideology is a direct attack on the modern liberal democratic state'.[10]

Writing from a very different point of view, Bernard Crick made a very sharp distinction between politics and ideology and identified the latter with totalitarianism:

> Totalitarian rule marks the sharpest contrast imaginable with political rule, and ideological thinking is an explicit and direct challenge to political thinking. The totalitarian believes that everything is relevant to government and that the task of government is to reconstruct society utterly according to the goals of an ideology.[11]

But it was in America that this identification of ideology and totalitarianism had been most clearly worked out, particularly by Hannah Arendt in her *Origins of Totalitarianism*.[12]

Here she delineated those specifically 'totalitarian elements that are peculiar to all ideological thinking': first, ideologies were not so much interested in what was the case as in the whole process of coming to be and passing away, in other words in a total explanation of all historical happenings; second, ideologies insist on a 'truth' behind that which is perceptible by the ordinary senses, a reality that requires for its detection a sixth sense only available to the initiate of the ideology; and, third, 'ideological thinking orders facts into an absolutely logical procedure which starts from an axiomatically accepted premise, deducing everything else from it; that is, it proceeds with a consistency that exists nowhere in the realm of reality'.[13] In sum, therefore,

> An ideology is quite literally what its name indicates; it is the logic of an idea. Its subject matter is history, to which the 'idea' is applied; the result of this application is not a body of statements about something that *is*, but the unfolding of a process which is in constant change. The ideology treats the course of events as though it followed the same 'law' as the logical exposition of its 'idea'. Ideologies pretend to know the mysteries of the whole historical process – the secrets of the past, the intricacies of the present, the uncertainties of the future – because of the logic inherent in their respective ideas.[14]

Since totalitarian politics became associated, in the post-war decades, with the Soviet Union, which was held to be Marxism in practice, the end of the ideology thesis often amounted to a thesis about the end of Marxism – 'the last great ideology' in Aron's words – and its irrelevance to advanced industrial societies.

The second, and rather broader, assumption lying behind the thesis was that it was possible to contrast ideology with science. 'Science' here involves an appeal to empirical observation and a rigid separation of fact from values. In contrast to the historist tradition discussed in the previous chapter, the scientific method is one and the same in the natural and social sciences. Typical of this approach are the two articles on ideology in the *International Encyclopaedia of the Social Sciences*. In the first article, Edward Shils allows that advances in scientific knowledge have been influenced by ideological thinking. But the progress of science involves an erosion of ideology. For, he continues,

> science is not and never has been part of an ideological culture. Indeed, the spirit in which science works is alien to ideology ... In so far as the social sciences have been genuinely intellectual pursuits, which have their own rules of judgement and observation and are open to criticism and revision, they are antipathetic to ideology.[15]

And his colleague Harry Johnson goes as far as to construct a definition of ideology in which 'ideology consists *only* of those parts or aspects of a system of social ideas which are distorted or unduly selective from a scientific point of view.'[16] This is firmly in the positivist tradition going back to Bacon's discussion of idols and de Tracy's construction of his science of ideas. Its most sophisticated recent exponent is Karl Popper who, although he would reject the label positivist, holds to a unified methodology for both natural and social sciences and to an appeal to immediate empirical observation to falsify hypotheses. Popper has used this methodology to attack Plato, Hegel and Marx as political theorists whose ideas are based on the dangerously ideological methods described by Hannah Arendt.[17]

The very bases of the mainstream American approach to the question of ideology have, naturally, come under heavy attack. There are some (of whom more in the next chapter) who have questioned the whole Enlightenment tradition of putting trust in reason and science as a force making almost inherently for social progress. For many of the Frankfurt School of social theorists, for example, the divide between natural and social science has broken down. In the words of its most extreme exponent: 'the very concept of technical reason is perhaps ideological. Not only the application of technology but technology itself is domination (of nature and men) methodic, scientific, calculated, calculating control.'[18] Thus there was no point in opposing science to ideology since science was itself ideological. Without going as far as that, it has frequently been pointed out how difficult it is to construct empirical and would-be value-free analyses without imparting some kind of ideological bias. All too often analyses of ideology are offered which brand the thoughts and beliefs of others as ideology, while not recognizing that their own analysis might rest on a framework which is equally vulnerable. The best way of illustrating this will be to take two fairly typical and specific examples in some detail. The purpose of having a closer look at these works is not to prove them mistaken but only to suggest that they are more ideological than their self-description would allow for.

The first example, appropriately, is a substantial article on ideology which has affinities with the 'end of ideology' school. In this article Giovanni Sartori aims to outline a concept of ideology that will be capable of serving as an analytical tool. As such, he tries to specify the nature of ideology in political belief systems and he contrasts ideology with pragmatism. Ideological belief systems spring from a cultural matrix which is rationalist; pragmatic belief systems spring from cultural matrices whose basis is empiricism. Thus ideology is impermeable to information which does not derive from an authoritative source within the ideology. By contrast, the pragmatic mentality is open-minded and tends to evaluate information on its own merits. The ideological mentality, therefore, 'can be legitimately understood to mean not only a rigid and dogmatic approach to politics, but also a principled and doctrinaire perception of politics'.[19] In addition, an ideological system has a high emotive content. Ideologies also have three other properties: they are articulate in that their concepts are explicit and contain a large number of elements; they are 'strongly constraining' in that these elements are 'tightly related in a quasi-logical fashion';[20] and, lastly, the first two properties mean that the holding of ideologies is confined to a relatively small minority. It follows that ideologies are articulate, highly constraining and held by an élite, while the beliefs of the masses have fewer elements and are altogether less sophisticated. Sartori's conclusion is:

the hetero-constraining potentiality of belief systems increases the more the system is ideological and diminishes the more the system is pragmatic. In short, ideologies are the *hetero-constraining* belief systems par excellence. And this is the same as saying that ideologies are the crucial lever at the disposal of elites for obtaining political mobilization and for maximizing the possibilities of mass manipulation. That is, it seems to me, the single major reason that ideology is so important to us. We are concerned about ideologies because we are concerned, in the final analysis, with the powers of man over man, with how populations and nations can be mobilized and manipulated all along the way that leads to political messianism and fanaticism.[21]

What are we to make of this? From the brief summary it will be clear that, although Sartori's analysis is offered as a contribution to empirical political theory,[22] the whole framework is heavily value-laden: a very strong value-position flows out of the analysis. This can be seen in three broad areas. First, by narrowing the concept of ideology – in order, allegedly, to give it some empirical purchase – it implies that there are some views, and in particular views which severely restrict the scope of the concept of ideology, which are not themselves ideological. Second, and more specifically, Sartori rejects the charge that his definition of ideology represents an anti-ideological bias. He does indeed define the ideological mentality as the rigid and dogmatic product of a closed mind, but maintains at the same time that 'ideological closeness is bad and pragmatic openness is good only according to an intellectual yardstick – and one could well say an intellectualistic prejudice'.[23] But this is surely disingenuous: the terms of the definition are strongly normative and do bias us inevitably against ideology. It is *not* simply a matter of 'intellectual prejudice' as to whether one is for or against rigidity, dogmatism and a closed mind. One could just as well defend calling someone a bastard on the grounds that such a description could be construed as laudatory – and if anyone chose to consider it differently this was simply due to prejudice. Third, ideology is here closely associated with totalitarianism – the views of Arendt and Friedrich cited above are quoted in this context. Even more explicitly, Marxism is referred to as the typical ideology, and liberalism is said to be a 'poor competitor, ideologically speaking, of socialism, communism, egalitarianism and the like'.[24] The upshot of this is inescapably to recommend one set of political doctrines over others. Fourth, Sartori allows ideologies only an emotive content thus implying that they have no cognitive content: they are merely expressions of approbation or disapprobation which are 'causes' or 'triggering mechanisms' for actions. This, again, is to devalue ideologies in line with the previous points. It could easily be argued, on the contrary, that the significance of ideology in mobilization is not that it 'causes one to do' but that it 'gives one cause for doing'. It provides grounds or warrants for the political activity engaged in. Reference to purposes and evaluations gives meaning to political actions, making them comprehensible to oneself and others. To explain the mobilizing aspects of ideology in terms of triggering mechanisms or the release of 'ideological passion', therefore, ignores a vast and important aspect of how political actors understand and orient their political activities, and how observers, attempting to understand these activities, might explain their significance.[25] But to adopt such an attitude would be to take the content of ideology much more seriously than Sartori is prepared to do. Finally, the view that 'mass publics are likely to display, in whatever country, a poorly explicated, inarticulate, disconnected – and therefore relatively unconstraining – belief system'[26] leads to the conclusion that 'mass beliefs appear to be dependent variables of elite belief policies'[27] and that 'mass publics are, in general, hetero-constrained, in the sense that poorly articulated believers need guidance not only for the horizontal inter-belief linkage, but also for the event-principle linkage.'[28] The implicit conclusion must be that most people are easily misled (as they have been typically in the Soviet Union) and that any society is better off without ideologies, all of which have dangerous inherent tendencies towards political messianism and fanaticism. In other words, any society – and in particular the industrial societies of the West – would be better off without any radicals. This may be true but it cannot be true simply in virtue of any theory which is empirical.

The second example of covert ideological bias is the way in which theories of American society as pluralist are often put forward as being more or less straightforward accounts of how things are – descriptive theories, therefore, with no evaluative content. Pluralism can be conceived of as a middle road between the theory of a power élite and classical democratic theory. The power élite theorists claim that America is controlled by a single élite which controls all major decisions; the classical democratic image is that of a society in which the majority of individuals make the most important decisions. In contrast to both of these views, a pluralist theory claims that political power is diffused in American society in that it is based on a number of factors such as wealth, status, official position, or voting power. Groups or individuals whose political influence depends on one factor have to compete for political power with groups or individuals having a different base. Contrary to the theory of the power élite, no one group has a monopoly of political power, and, contrary to classical democracy, political decisions are seldom, if ever, the result of the wish of the majority, but result from competition between different centres of power.

Pluralism is more similar, however, to the classical model, in that it substitutes the groups engendered by modern industrial society for the isolated individuals as the basic unit of social interaction. This system has been described by one of its most lucid exponents as 'polyarchy', a system in which minorities rule in the sense that the competition of political parties for elective support reflects the pressures of various organized minorities. The system is an open one in that any organized and legal group can expect to have its point of view seriously considered by those taking political decisions. In the end, politics comes down to bargaining. Nevertheless, in *A Preface to Democratic Theory* (1956) R. Dahl writes:

> if the majority rarely rules on matters of specific policy, the specific policies selected by a process of 'minorities rule' probably lie most of the time within the bounds of consensus set by the important values of the politically active members of the society, of whom the voters are a key group.[29]

Thus it is also possible to claim that the majority does rule, in that 'politicians subject to elections must operate within limits set both their own values as indoctrinated members of society, and by their expectations of what policies they can adopt and still be re-elected'.[30] What is ordinarily understood as politics – election campaigns, differing party programmes, etc. – represents merely superficial conflicts. The emphasis in pluralist theory is rather on the underlying consensus: 'prior to politics, beneath it, enveloping it, restricting it, conditioning it, is the underlying consensus on policy that usually exists in the society among a predominant portion of the politically active members.[31]

In what way, then, does the pluralist view, which sets itself out as being a descriptive view with which every close observer of the political scene could agree, contain an ideology in Mannheim's sense of a perspective with which those adopting a different perspective could legitimately disagree? In so far as the pluralist model emphasizes the formal decision-making process, it must neglect the non-decision-making process by which what might become public issues never emerge as such. Pluralism assumes that the important issues are those which take place in the public arena of formal procedure. But, as has been pointed out,

> the pluralists suppose that because power, as they conceptualise it, only shows up in cases of actual conflict, it follows that actual conflict is necessary to power, but this is to ignore the crucial point that the most effective and insidious use of power is to prevent such conflict existing in the first place.[32]

And of course there is the point that if there is a winnowing out of issues beforehand, then there is also a toning down and re-interpretation of them afterwards. In his well-known study of politics in New Haven, Dahl examined the decision-making process with regard to several important issues. But how do we decide what is 'important'? The issues were chosen because 'they promised to cut across a wide variety of interests and participants. These were redevelopment, public education, and nominations in the two major parties'.[33] But the outcome of the investigation threatens to become self-confirming since these are exactly the sort of issues that would tend to be solved by the sort of bargaining that pluralism claims is characteristic of politics as a whole. A further difficulty in confining observation to observable decision-making processes is that often people will adjust their views and demands according to what they predict will be their effect on those in positions of power – which again means that some important issues and points of view may be ruled out by anticipation. Moreover, the pluralist assumption that everyone is able to know and articulate their interest is questionable. For if we take the view that people either may not be aware of their own interests or may misconceive them, then the claim of the pluralist world to be representative of, and responsive to, the interests of people, would be severely shaken.[34]

More fundamentally, the model of surface conflict and underlying consensus invokes an image of American society in which those in power simply apply to practical problems the values which are held in common. In this view of power as the collective product of society (a view most influentially presented in the sociology of Talcott Parsons), relations of power are reciprocal and realized mainly through authority and bargaining, both of which are sustained by a general commitment to the 'rules of the game'. But power could equally well be viewed as a zero-sum: if someone has a given amount of power, then someone else has concomitantly less. And if power is a scare commodity, then coercion and manipulation are liable to be more important than authority and bargaining. Moreover, although it might be agreed that there was such a consensus supporting the present power structure, it could equally be argued that it is a power élite which shapes the consensus since it also benefits most from it.

In effect, what pluralists are doing is to change the connotations of the word 'democracy' and make the concept compatible with, if not actually constituted by, a more conservative view of society. For the narrowing down of what constitutes rule by the people undoubtedly devalues the idea of popular participation. Thus the pluralist theory 'is in reality deeply rooted in an ideology, an ideology which is grounded upon a profound distrust of the majority of ordinary men and women and a reliance upon the established élites to maintain the values of civility and the "rules of the game" of democracy'.[35] Pluralism can also be seen, more generously, as an instance of Durkheim's account of ideology: it is the 'civil religion' of a society with no feudal past, a society which can seem classless in that its members were, in de Toqueville's phrase, 'born free'.

Dahl's model, therefore, of surface competition between interest groups founded on an underlying social consensus involves a particular view or perspective on politics. These two crucial variables – surface competition and underlying consensus – are being presented as the necessary conditions for democracy. But democracy is a concept with unavoidably normative overtones, and what purports to be a generalization from the experience of American politics turns into a recommendation of the status quo. This does not mean that pluralism is necessarily false or mistaken only that it does not have the obvious authority that would attend a descriptive or factual statement.

Empirical investigations of ideology have produced considerable information about the beliefs people hold, particularly in areas connected with mass communications, social psychology and voting behaviour. The extensive nature of these findings has been in proportion to the size of the resources and personnel available to these fields. But this mass of information (useful as most of it undoubtedly is) has not been matched by progress with theories as to how to order it to make it meaningful. Too many social scientists have sought to bracket the philosophical problems inherent in their research. This has been all the easier in the United States where the role of ideology has been less evident, though more pervasive, than elsewhere. It has often been pointed out, not least by Habermas, that capitalism seems to operate all by itself and without the need for any ideological justification in that its commodities and markets generate their own compelling logic. As we have seen, however, to step out of the ideological circle is more difficult than many are prepared to admit. Contemporary attempts to face this problem head-on are the subject of the next chapter.

Science, Language and Ideology

The analyses of ideology considered in the preceding chapter depend on the opposition between ideology and some sort of science. For much of mainstream Anglo-Saxon social science is continuing the tradition of de Tracy's science of ideas, a tradition which broadly goes under the label of positivism. Although there are many different sorts of positivism, there is general agreement among positivists that the social sciences should model themselves on the natural sciences, whose mode of procedure is the only one thought capable of producing valid knowledge. This valid social science must be strongly empirical by appealing to an objective world of facts and its method is one of rejecting all conceptions that cannot, in principle, be verified (or at least falsified) by appealing to such facts.

However, this assimilation of the social to the natural world has come under attack from those who question whether natural science (let alone social science) is quite as objective and neutral as is widely believed. Such people would not wish to deny that the vast emphasis of recent decades on empirical social science has indeed provided us with a lot of potential information about society, but would claim that there remains a still vaster problem of interpretation. It is obvious that to equate social facts with natural facts is to invest social facts with the same air of immutability that attaches to nature and thus has distinctly conservative implications. But some critics of positivism wish to go further and suggest that not only is there no sharp distinction between science and ideology, but that much of natural science is itself ideological. This disquiet over the status of natural science is prompted by the failure of scientific advance to deliver the blessings that many in the last century expected: the emergence of the ecological and anti-nuclear movements are only the most evident examples of this disquiet.

The best-known advocate of this view was Herbert Marcuse, but he shared the suspicion of natural science and the technology that accompanies it with Max Horkheimer and Theodor Adorno, who together formed the most prominent members of the Frankfurt School. While strongly influenced, at least originally, by Marx, they thought of Marxism as having been substantially misled by the Enlightenment's confidence in scientific reason and the consequential view of the growth of the productive forces as inherently progressive. According to Horkheimer, with the prestige of science, the use of reason had become almost exclusively 'instrumental'. In the great philosophical systems of the past, however misguided, at least there was debate about the ends of human life. Nowadays, reason had been reduced to technical talk about means, discussion about ends being the realm of propaganda. Debate about the goals of society had been occluded by the industrialization of reason, by its becoming the handmaiden of technical domination. Scientific method was held up as a norm, but, according to Horkheimer:

> Science has no realistic grasp of that comprehensive relationship upon which its own existence and the direction of its work depend, namely, society. . . . For Science, too, is determined in the scope and direction of its work not by its own tendencies alone but, in the last analysis, by social life as well.[1]

This attack on the supposed neutrality of science and its rise as a model for rational thought reached its extreme in Marcuse's best-selling *One-Demensional Man* whose central thesis was that

> the closed operational universe of advanced industrial civilization with its terrifying harmony of freedom and oppression, productivity and destruction, growth and regression is pre-designed in this idea of Reason as a specific historical project. The technological and pre-technological stages share certain basic concepts of man and nature which express the continuity of the Western tradition. Within this continuum, different modes of thought clash with each other; they belong to different ways of apprehending, organizing, changing society and nature. The stabilizing tendencies conflict with the subversive elements of Reason, the power of positive with that of

negative thinking, until the achievements of advanced industrial
civilization lead to the triumph of the one-dimensional reality over all
contradictions.[2]

Thus the destructive nature of instrumental reason called for a
society based on other principles – though Marcuse was, naturally,
not in a position to describe how such a society would come about
and still less how it would operate.

A similar questioning of the status of natural science (though
without the pessimistic conclusions of the Frankfurt School) has
come from two Anglo-Saxon philosophers of science. Thomas
Kuhn in his influential book *The Structure of Scientific Revolutions*
contested the traditional empirical and rational image of science as
a steady accumulation of agreed facts which progressively un-
covered the real nature of the world. On the contrary, according to
Kuhn, science proceeded by imaginative leaps and bounds from one
'paradigm' to another. A paradigm was instituted by 'universally
recognized scientific achievements that for a time provide model
problems and solutions to a community of practitioners'.[3] In time,
every paradigm proved insufficient to accommodate discrepancies
and anomalies whereupon one or more new paradigms would be
proposed. Although Kuhn never went as far as claiming that there
were no objective grounds for deciding between competing paradigms, he did stress that it was not a simple matter of experimentation and appeal to evidence. A more extreme proponent of the
a-rationality of scientific method is Paul Feyerabend, who claims
that the idea that natural science contains knowledge independent
of ideology, social prejudice, etc., is simply a 'fairy tale' – there
being no essential difference between natural science and the claims
of mysticism or religion.

Although the ideas of Feyerabend do touch the wilder shores of
relativism, there has been widespread criticism over the last two
decades of the idea both that natural science is unproblematically
objective and that the methods of the natural sciences can be
applied to the social sciences.[4] But during the same period a method
for analysis in the social sciences has risen to prominence which
claims, on quite different grounds, to be scientific and which has
obvious implications for the study of ideology. This is the method of
structuralism.

Structuralism has its origin in the study of linguistics. Almost a century ago the Swiss linguist Ferdinand Saussure distinguished between *language* and *speech*. Language is a formal system (or structure) of arbitrary signs which are related to one another and which underlie all speech. The laws of language, i.e. the laws of structural linguistics, are not the laws of every day human speech: they are rather the laws of unmotivated, conventional categories of which the speaker is unconscious and powerless to alter. It is this underlying and unchanging system or structure which can be studied with scientific precision in abstraction from the superficial speech patterns which individuals may choose to adopt. By extension all social and intellectual activity can best be understood by referring it to an underlying system of meaning. It is easy to see the parallel with psychoanalysis. For in a manner reminiscent of Freudian psychoanalysis, a distinction is drawn between manifest content and latent content: the manifest content is the ordinary speech or activities of individuals, the latent content is the hidden structure of this speech or activity. And just as in Freud the 'slip' is to be explained by reference to the unconscious and its repressed contents, so the actual discourse or activities of individuals can be viewed as a screen hiding the underlying ideological structure of their words or actions.

Structuralism has had a considerable impact in anthropology and particularly the study of myth, so let us briefly consider the major thinker in this field, Claude Levi-Strauss, as an example, before considering in more detail the possible relation of language and ideology. Levi-Strauss uses the opposition of basic infrastructure to the conscious use of language to examine the role of myth. For him, mythical thinking, and cultural phenomena in general, are a sort of language in which societies express themselves in diverse ways but always according to the systematic universal laws of the unconscious structure. This underlying structure is both necessary and eternal and is the starting point for any account of human society. As an illustration of the primary nature of structures, Levi-Strauss likens them to the rules of a card-game: every game of cards is different since the number of possible variations is, for all practical purposes, infinite. But each game is strictly governed by the underlying rules which never vary and prescribe exactly which combinations are, and which are not, possible.

The idea of structural determinism has, according to Levi-Strauss, wide applicability. In the modern age, mythology is to be sought in political ideology – he refers to the French Revolution – and even in science itself. For the world of contemporary natural science and the world of myth yield two 'distinct though equally positive sciences'. It is only now that these two separate paths to knowledge unite: 'that which arrives at the physical world by the detour of communication, and that which, as we have recently come to know, arrives at the world of communication by the detour of the physical. The entire process of human knowledge thus assumes the character of a closed system'.[5] The same inbuilt cultural universal, the same logical system, underlies both and provides the only means of explicating them.

The structuralist approach to the study of myth certainly reveals connections that have stimulated the imagination of anthropologists. When it comes to considering ideology, the ideas of Levi-Strauss seem too general, since by privileging form over content and logical classification over practical results, it becomes difficult to distinguish between fact and imagination, between science, religion and myth. Levi-Strauss claims to show 'not how men think in myths but how myths operate in men's minds without their being aware of the fact'.[6] This is to reduce the whole of the conscious individual in a manner which goes far beyond even the psychoanalysis of Freud. Moreover, by explicating all intellectual activity in terms of a common structure, it is to emphasize the consensual element in human affairs at the expense of the conflictual.

However, the same schema of underlying structure determining surface phenomena has been applied – with the same would-be scientific rigour – to the connection between language and ideology. Previously language had been rather taken for granted, like a window through which we look at the world outside. The recent prestige of linguistics, itself the product of a hi-tech information society, has led to attention being paid to language itself: instead of simply looking through the glass, we look at it, since the shape of the window or the arrangement of the panes may determine what we see through them. On this view, ideology may go well beyond the scope of language as ordinarily conceived. For the study of linguistics leads us to suppose that other forms of human activity can be construed as languages, i.e. as systems of signs which have a meaning.

In any system of signs, according to the structuralist view, there is, as we have seen, a distinction between *speech* and *language*.

Speech is the manifest level, the one that is immediately apparent; language is the latent level, the hidden structure. It is in language that ideology is to be found. The ideological message is contained in the underlying structure, which is so packaged in speech as to be more or less inaccessible to both speakers and hearers. One of the most lucid, influential and readable exponents of this view, Roland Barthes, expresses this as a distinction between what a statement *denotes* and what it *connotes*. A famous example of this is the humorous reporting of a so-called 'blue-blood' cruise in which many royal personages gathered on a yacht for a trip round the Mediterranean. The public was vastly amused, but, says Barthes:

> Such a feeling of amusement carries a heavy pathological burden; if one is amused by a contradiction, it is because one supposes its terms to be very far apart. In other words, kings have a superhuman essence, and when they temporarily borrow certain forms of democratic life, it can only be through an incarnation which goes against nature, made possible through condescension alone. To flaunt the fact that kings are capable of prosaic actions is to recognize that this status is no more natural to them than angelism to common mortals, it is to acknowledge that the king is still king by divine right.[7]

In other words, when kings play at being men, what is *denoted* is their human side, but this only serves to *connote* their superhuman attributes.

In recent years there have been many attempts to give an account of the relation of language to ideology in structuralist terms, which are generally described as 'discourse analysis' and intended to have a critical edge to them. Elaborating on such cryptic remarks of Marx as 'language *is* practical, real consciousness',[8] discourse analysis takes as its subject the language of everyday life, the language of newspapers, magazines, classrooms, families, and it analyses the patterns of sentences in extended pieces of prose or in conversational exchanges. It also attempts less successfully to show how these patterns reflect relations of power on the grounds, again, that language is a form of activity – just as many forms of activity can be interpreted as languages. This goes further than the evident ideological context which informs the description of guerrilla forces as either 'freedom fighters' or 'terrorists'. It aims to uncover ideological implications in the apparently innocent structure of sentences. Some of these analyses yield little more than lists of categories, others try, more fruitfully, to connect their analyses to social relations. A simple example of this might be the sentence, 'The warder marched the prisoners', which can be broken down into (A) The warder caused X and (B) The prisoners marched. According to analyses of this sort,

> The actor of A becomes the imputed actor for the new sentence. The assumption that underlies the process is that power can be regarded as direct agency. The effect of this linguistic process is to reassign the actor roles in the two conflated models. The real actor of the process is denied credit and responsibility for the action he performs, and this credit is assigned to the syntactic participant who is regarded as more powerful. It is a thing not lightly done. The ideological function is clear.[9]

This may seem simply to be reconveying in terms of linguistic analysis what we all know prison life to be like anyway. But other, less obvious examples would be the frequent use of agentless passives ('The government has been criticized'), which by deleting reference to any agent deflects the force of the criticism, or the use of abstract nouns ('criticism of the government has been increased') which have the same effect. This is to give a critical edge to Chomsky's notion of transformation grammar:

> Below the surface of an utterance, in this view, are successive layers of structure, variously transformed or classified. A hearer or reader can attempt to recover these until the underlying set of basic forms is reached. Full decoding, then, is a journey into these depths, following in reverse the hypothesized genesis of the utterance: a description of the underlying forms, and a precise history of what has happened to them.[10]

With these latter analyses we have moved beyond structuralism to a kind of sociolinguistics.

If the concept of ideology is to have any critical edge, then structuralist principles require severe modification. Those principles have encountered three main difficulties. The first, and most evident, is that the meaning of a piece of writing is not to be deciphered simply by looking – however hard – at the words and sentences. Analysis that is strictly confined to the text breaks it down into units and then constructs models which are both drastic oversimplifications and often arbitrary. In a modern version of old idealist doctrines, discourse analysis sometimes seems to imply that only signs exist and that the universe is an endless round of signifiers with nothing signified: we cannot look through the window but remain condemned to stare at the glass. But the meaning of any set of words depends heavily on the conditions under which it is produced and those under which it is received by its readers or hearers. Language is a form of action and, like most forms of action, its efficiency depends very heavily on the context. Prime examples of this are the so-called 'performative' utterances, whereby the speaker performs an action by uttering certain words – for example, by saying 'I promise' in a marriage ceremony the speaker performs the act of getting married. But the meaning and effectiveness of the words depends on a whole set of institutional arrangements and presuppositions: it is not possible for just anyone to open a motorway by snipping some red tape and saying 'I open', or to condemn someone to death by putting on a black cap and saying 'I sentence'.[11] A different way of making the same general point would be to say the statements are *about* something, they suggest something, and to understand them is to understand their relationship to what they are about, i.e. to the world outside the statement. Irony, for example, is very difficult to discover without knowledge of the circumstances of a statement. Thus the meaning of a statement is bound up with its function, with what it *does*, and reference to the world outside the statement is essential to this: text is dependent on context.

A different sort of difficulty is that emphasis on the autonomy of *language* over speech removes it from social and historical influences. There is no evidence for the existence of independent rules of syntax lying behind speech and governing what can, or at least what cannot, be said. For as soon as such rules are stated it is possible in theory at least – and sometimes in practice – to find examples of their modification by social and historical circumstances.

A further criticism of structural approaches in general is that they tend to emphasize the consensual rather than the conflictual aspects of society and thus tend to legitimate the social order rather than to criticize it. For a structure is something objective and defines bounds beyond which we cannot step. It points to an underlying consensus in which we are all implicated. This is a version of the idea that in every society there is a dominant ideology in the shape of a coherent set of principles meeting general acceptance and serving to legitimate existing relations of power. This view has been highly

contested. In anthropology the opinion of Edmund Leach that
'myth and ritual is a language of signs in terms of which claims to
rights and status are expressed, but it is a language of argument, not
a chorus of harmony'[12] is obviously at variance with the views of
Levi-Strauss. In medieval society it might be claimed that the
dominant politico-religious ethos served more to reinforce the
esprit de corps of the ruling groups than to legitimate them in the
eyes of the mass of the people who were either ignorant of, or
indifferent to, this ethos.[13] In contemporary Western society there
are many who claim that what stability it has depends not so much
on any underlying consensus among its members but more on its
fragmentation. As with the view of medieval society mentioned
above, the acceptance of the values and norms of 'liberal democracy' are strongest among those at the top of the social scale: those
at the bottom have no coherent or cohesive means to express their
disaffection.

   This point about consensus and conflict leads on to another
difficulty in the structuralist approach – the apparent disappearance
of the subject in the sense of a reflective, responsible and creative
agent, a process elaborated in the varieties of post-structuralist and
post-modernist writers examined in the next chapter. In reacting
against the excessive subjectivity of existentialism with its emphasis
on the absolute freedom and responsibility of every person,
structuralism has gone to the other extreme. It is one thing to realize
how bounded that freedom is by the structures of language and of
society, and it is quite another to dissolve the subject into those
same social relations and linguistic forms. More specifically, any
understanding, whether of action or words, seems to involve the
process of interpretation which implies a creative subjectivity. The
would-be objective and scientifically determinable nature of structures can never be so overwhelming as to squeeze out entirely the
subjective element in human action.

   In sum, there is no doubt that the emphasis on language with its
distinction between denotation and connotation has provided new
insights. And obviously there is great importance in the kind of
sociolinguistics which demonstrates how political, social or sexual
prejudice is reinforced by language. But the hope that these could
be formulated within the confines of a general scientific theory of
structuralist inspiration has proved unfounded. For the underlying
structures seem on inspection to be no different from the older idea

of philosophical world-views between which no science can act as arbiter.

In order to draw together the threads of what has been rather a disparate discussion, let us look briefly at Jurgen Habermas, probably the most influential contemporary thinker in this area. Habermas has attempted, by drawing on the latest discussions in sociology, linguistics and many other areas to construct an analysis of society in which the concept of ideology would preserve its critical edge. The best way of introducing the complex thought of Habermas is to see what he borrows from the accounts of ideology we have already discussed.

Clearly, Habermas is much indebted to Marx. He accepts much of Marx's materialist conception of history in which the historical material conditions under which human labour has occurred have set the developing parameters for knowledge. Marx, according to Habermas, sets his conception of history in the context of a dialectic between the tools and instruments that human beings have at their disposal at any given time – the forces of production – and the institutional arrangements with their cultural and symbolic accompaniments. However, Habermas thinks that there is a tendency in Marx to over-emphasize the former:

> the productive activity which regulates the material exchange of the human species with its natural environment, becomes the paradigm for the generation of all the categories, everything is resolved into the self-movement of production. Because of this, Marx's brilliant insight into the dialectical relationship between the forces of production and the relations of production could very quickly be misinterpreted in a mechanistic manner.[14]

This tendency to emphasize economic determinism and assimilate the social to the natural sciences was taken much further by Engels, Bukharin and others. Habermas, by contrast, while not wishing to deny the importance of material labour and the technical innovations through which its forms develop, wants also to stress the importance of cultural tradition and institutional arrangements – which together he often refers to as 'interaction'. Unlike Marx – and more particularly unlike many of Marx's orthodox successors – Habermas claims that there is no 'automatic developmental relation between labour and interaction'.[15]

This attention to non-economic factors and the need for a drastic reformulation of Marx is justified, according to Habermas, by the changes in advanced industrial society over the last 100 years. He thinks that whereas in Marx's time the prevailing ideology was based on the idea of equal exchange in the market, the advance of technology in the twentieth century has given rise to a technocratic consciousness which reduces the political to the technical. The increasing intervention of the state in social and economic affairs has meant an equally increasing number of administrators and experts to take decisions based on the needs of the technocratic system: this involves a change in the ideology appropriate to such a society which moves from a consideration of just exchange and equality to justifying decisions in terms of technical questions appropriate to science and industry. This process involves at the same time a depoliticization of society. While being in a sense less ideological than its predecessors in that it does not represent an idealization or illusion over against 'real' life, this technocratic consciousness is at the same time more ideological: for it is both more pervasive and harder to oppose than its predecessors in that it simply suppresses all possible alternatives in the name of economy and efficiency and only allows debate to take place about different means to a predetermined end. Thus, while not going all the way with Marcuse in his condemnation of industrial society, Habermas is strongly inspired by this line of thought.

The distinction between labour and interaction involved a much enlarged conception of the crisis of capitalist society. Whereas Marx considered crisis mainly in economic terms, Habermas outlined a whole typology of crises inherent in late capitalism: an economic crisis, a crisis of rationality, of legitimacy, and of motivation. In Habermas's view, an economic crisis in late capitalism was not inevitable. But the steps taken by the state to avert it entailed a crisis of rationality. For the conflict of interests inherent in late capitalism and the contradictory demands on state intervention tended to mean that state aid was dysfunctionally distributed. This in turn created a crisis of legitimacy, for state intervention meant opening up the question of control and choice. The only solutions were buying off the most powerful parties or the creation of a new legitimizing ideology. In addition, growing public intervention involved lessening the scope of the private sphere which had motivated bourgeois society and thereby a crisis in motivation which had hitherto depended on the idea of the market as a fair distributor of values. Summarizing his conclusions, Habermas declared:

> Economic crises are shifted into the political system through the reactive-avoidance activity of the government in such a way that supplies of legitimation can compensate for deficits in rationality and extensions of organisational rationality can compensate for those legitimation deficits that do appear. There arises a bundle of crisis tendencies that, from a genetic point of view, represents a hierarchy of crisis phenomena shifted upwards from below. But from the point of view of governmental crisis management, these crisis phenomena are distinguished by being mutually substitutable within certain limits. These limits are determined by, on the one hand, the fiscally available quantity of value – the shortage of which cannot be validly predicted within crisis theory – and on the other by supplies of motivation from the socio-cultural system. The substitutive relation between the scarce resources, value and meaning, is therefore decisive for the prediction of crisis.[16]

This expanded idea of crisis and the relativizing of the economic sphere involved a drastic reformulation of Marx's historical materialism. Clearly Habermas's ideas have strong affinities with those of the Frankfurt School. His whole revision of Marx is governed by the School's criticism of instrumental reason, the scientific or technical reason which had come to dominate society in the twentieth century. Besides a legitimate interest in the instrumental reason which served to control objectified processes, Habermas claimed that human beings had two other interests: a practical interest in communicating with each other in forms of social organization and an interest in being self-reflective and self-determining, i.e. an emancipatory interest in autonomy. Also, like many members of the Frankfurt School, Habermas is interested in Freudian psychoanalysis as a model of emancipation. He thinks there are strong parallels between the development of the individual according to Freud and the development of the human species. Just as an individual whose ego organization is weak will find a neurotic solution to certain forms of inner repression, so societies generate ideologies which are rationalizations of asymmetrical power relations which have been repressed, elided or distorted in language. And just as the Freudian analyst leads the patient to self-awareness, so critical theory can do the same for a society by exposing the roots of its legitimating ideology.

The novel element in Habermas's theory of ideology is his emphasis on language. Like most writers influenced by the Western Marxist tradition, Habermas wishes to stress the importance of the superstructure as opposed to the rather rigid economic determinism of classical Marxism. But for him the key to the superstructure lies in language, in that 'today the problem of language has replaced the traditional problem of consciousness.'[17] His concentration on language, however, is far from being disembodied. It is closely linked to a study of society in that he believes that language not only constitutes social phenomena but is itself constituted (and distorted) by them. The study of ideology is therefore the study of systematically distorted communication.

What is distinctive about Habermas's interest in language is how he proposes to establish a criterion by which to judge ideology. If this enterprise involves the explanation of systematically distorted communication then it must also involve the 'mastery of the idea of undistorted communication or reasonable discourse'.[18] And this idea, he claims, is implicit in any use of language. For the very act of speech involves the supposition of the possibility of an ideal speech situation in which the force of the better argument alone will decide the issue. For people speaking to each other aim at reaching some kind of understanding. Communicative interaction presupposes that those engaging in it could sustain four types of validity claim: first, that what they say is comprehensible; second, that it is true; third, that it is legitimate in the context; and last, that it is sincerely meant. The redemption of these claims is only possible if all members of society have an equal chance to participate in the discussion; and this involves the notion of the transformation of society in a direction that would enable such a communicative competence to characterize all members of society. For technological society can only be rational if its policies are subject to public control. But, for this to happen, discussion and opinion have to be free from manipulation and domination. The ultimate goal of social emancipation is, therefore, inherent in any and every speech act.

In contemporary society there exist profound barriers to this 'discursive will-formation'. For

> The validity of [contemporary] world-views is secured in a communi-
> cation structure which excludes discursive will-formation ... the
> barriers to communication which make a fiction precisely of the
> reciprocal imputation of accountability, support at the same time the
> belief in legitimacy that sustains the fiction and prevents its being
> found out. That is the paradoxical achievement of ideologies, whose
> individual prototype is the neurotic disturbance.[19]

This approach allows us to gauge the extent of ideology in any
society by counterposing to the actual state of affairs the question:

> how would the members of a social system, at a given stage of
> development of productive forces, have collectively and bindingly
> interpreted their needs (and which norms would they have accepted
> as justified) if they could and would have decided on the organization
> of social intercourse through discursive will-formation, with ad-
> equate knowledge of the limiting conditions and functional impera-
> tives of their society?[20]

Thus Habermas wishes to conclude that his criticism of ideology is
not arbitrary but is 'inherent in the very structure of social action
and language' into which, in their turn, most values are inextricably
woven:

> Only in an emancipated society, whose members' autonomy and
> responsibility had been realized, would communication have de-
> veloped into the non-authoritarian and universally practiced dia-
> logue from which both our model of reciprocally constituted ego
> identity and our idea of true consensus are always implicitly derived.
> To this extent the truth of statements is based on anticipating the
> realization of the good life.[21]

It is not surprising that Habermas's wide-ranging ideas have
raised several objections. The parallel Habermas is keen to draw
between psychoanalysis and social liberation is suspect both
because it involves an illegitimate move from the individual to the
social and also because in psychoanalysis the process is one of
willing co-operation, whereas this is unlikely to be the case in
liberation from social domination. More centrally, the equation of
ideology with distorted communication is not specific enough since
not all distorted communication is ideological. The whole concentration of language and communicative competence seems to
neglect material domination and class interest: access to unfettered

communication may not be enough to secure an emancipated society if access to wealth and status are not similarly equalized. But, however formal and abstract much of his presentation may be, Habermas has succeeded in uniting the themes of science, language and ideology more interestingly than any other contemporary thinker.

7

Ideology and the 'End of History'

Both structuralism and the very different approach of Habermas have recently come under attack from the increasingly influential view of the world known as postmodernism. Postmodernism is almost as elusive a concept as ideology itself.[1] This is because – like the terms post-Christian, post-Marxist, post-structuralism – it defines itself negatively. Critical and mockingly destructive, it rejects even very broad and tentative attempts to find some foundation for our thought. It turns all our 'isms' into 'wasms' and resolutely turns its back on efforts to give some overall account of our nature and destiny: it wishes to be post-everything, elevates incoherence to its defining feature, and sees even reason itself as the mere tool of a Nietzschean will to power. All this sounds confusingly relativist. However, no thinkers, not even postmodernists, can be consistently relativists without disappearing completely up their own backsides. So the most useful approach will be to ask whether postmodernism is not itself an ideology which will, in turn, suggest that we look at the social and historical context in which it has arisen and flourishes.

Postmodernism is a reaction to, and an extension of, modernity. It is 'in every respect parasitic on modernity: it lives and feeds on its achievements and on its dilemmas'.[2] By 'modernity' here is meant the Enlightenment project of achieving increasing material and moral progress for humankind through the application of science and reason. This project, like the Christianity it was in many ways intended to supercede, involved an account of where we have come from, where we are going, how we can get there, and why we should bother to go. Building on the subversion of the whole of the

Western philosophical tradition to be found in writers such as
Nietzsche and Heidegger, Postmodernist thinkers are typically
sceptical of such universal schemes which they call 'meta-
narratives': they prefer to concentrate on smaller-scale accounts or
narratives and deny that such accounts can be united, and judged, in
terms of some over-arching account and judgement.

Postmodernist thinkers concentrate on three claims. First, according to a leading exponent such as Jacques Derrida, we have no
direct encounter with reality through reason, but only through our
images of it.[3] We construct our accounts of reality in words. Just as a
building consists in its bricks, so reality consists in the words, images
and metaphors that we use to describe it. By deconstructing the
picture that we have made of reality we lay bare its (lack of)
foundations. Thus 'today, culture impacts back on reality in ways
that make any independent and, as it were, non- or extra cultural
form of it problematical (in a kind of Heisenberg principle of mass
culture which intervenes between your eye and the thing itself), so
that finally the theorists unite their voices in the new doxa that the
'referent' no longer exists'.[4] There is a well-known story of an
ancient sage who was asked about the foundation of the world. He
replied that the world rested on an elephant. When asked what the
elephant rested on, he replied that it rested on a turtle and when
asked what the turtle rested on, he replied: 'it's turtles all the way
down.' In postmodernist thought we are in danger of losing nature
and reality completely and descending in a spiral of endless
metaphor. Second, the self is held to be no longer the confident and
sovereign being of much modernist thought. The self is no longer
the potential lord of all it surveys and capable of shaping history in
accordance with human aims. The self has been deconstructed or
decentred, typically in the work of Foucault whose studies on
attitudes to madness, the history of prisons and of sexuality claimed
to show how human individuality is itself historically constructed
and produced by all-pervasive impersonal relations of power. For
Foucault, 'man is an invention the recent date of which is easily
demonstrated by the archaeology of our thought, an invention
which is also perhaps near its end. If there were to occur in the
present times an intellectual revolution similar to that of the
Enlightenment then it would be odds on that man would be effaced
just like a picture drawn in the sand by the incoming tide'.[5] Third,
postmodernism celebrates the existence of difference, variety and

diversity for their own sakes. The effort to homogenize, to impose a false unity is characteristic of ideological thinking. Since there is no foundation or reality to which thought can be subjected and since even the self is divided in that the rational superego of Freud has given way to the amorphous and slippery Other of Lacan, there is no standpoint from which to impose a unity on the spontaneous diversity of existence.

The disappearance of a stable reality and of a stable conception of the self have obvious parallels with recent economic developments such as the anti-planning views that surfaced during the Reagan and Thatcher years. The dominance of the 'free' market led to an economic anarchy in which, in Marx's famous phrase, 'all that is solid melts into air'.[6] The impression of the lack of solidity in social and economic life was reinforced by the acceleration in the turnover time of capital fostered by the growth of information technology. This can be seen as the cultural logic of the late capitalism in which the 'information society' not only produces new theories of language but in which 'aesthetic production today has become integrated into commodity production generally: the frantic economic urgency of producing fresh waves of ever more novel-seeming goods (from clothing to aeroplanes), at ever greater rates of turnover, now assigns an increasingly essential structural function and position to aesthetic innovation and experimentation'.[7] In a society where packaging and imaging are crucial in the sale of politics as much as of beer, where time and space are increasingly compressed by information super-highways, where news reports are referred to as 'stories' and murderously armed nation states as 'players', it is not surprising that reality becomes virtual and people begin to lose any firm conception of their individualities.[8]

Some have seen postmodernism theories as subversive of old authoritarian ideologies and thus pointing to the emergence of an ultra-pluralist society in which different collective social practices could flourish. In this context the concept of civil society has made a striking return to political thought: the unifying state has failed as a moral project and civil society with its variety of institutions, clubs, professional associations and pressure groups is seen as the area where diversity can be fostered.[9] Others have suggested that the belief that all thought is ideological and merely the articulate expression of conflicting interests and desires is itself an ideology all of its own.[10] It confuses objectivity with disinterestedness – but we can have a very direct interest in finding out the truth. Postmodernism, by contrast, tends to give up on concepts such as truth which it dissolves into an interplay of rhetoric and power. By claiming that, since no one is disinterested, there is no such thing as objectivity but only an endless clash of perspectives, postmodernism seems, as Habermas has argued, to induce a scepticism and passivity which effectively favours a conservatism bolstering the *status quo*.[11] Moreover, some postmodernist writers, such as Baudrillard and Lyotard, tend to homogenize interests, to equate all desires and thus deprive themselves of saying which interests, desires and conflicts are more important than others: the interests of stamp-collectors and politicians are much the same.

Some have seen postmodernism as a recycling of the 'end of ideology' thesis discussed in Chapter 5. Postmodernism is certainly keen on ends in general. Indeed, as Jameson has remarked, postmodernism is constituted by 'an inverted millenarianism in which premonitions of the future, catastrophic or redemptive, have been replaced by senses of the end of this or that (the end of ideology, art, or social class; the 'crisis' of Leninism, social democracy, or the welfare state, etc., etc.)',[12] The end of ideology has recently been endorsed by Richard Rorty, the most prominent exponent of postmodernism in the United States. Rorty's playful and ironic liberalism springs from a postmodernism which expresses the continental European tradition of Nietzsche and Heidegger through an Anglo-Saxon analytical pragmatism. In his view, liberal democracy cannot have, and does not need, any philosophical justification. He believes that 'contemporary liberal society already contains the institutions for its own improvement – an improvement which can mitigate the dangers Foucault sees. Indeed, my hunch is that Western social and political thought may have had the last *conceptual* revolution it needs'.[13] In Rorty's view, echoing what he takes to be the later views of John Rawls, just liberal democracy 'will be a society which encourages the "end of ideology", that takes reflective equilibrium as the only method needed in discussing social policy. When such a society deliberates, when it collects the principles and the intuitions to be brought into equilibrium, it will tend to discard those drawn from philosophical accounts of the self, of rationality'.[14] Rorty's appeal here to 'our' common intuitions and traditional practices is reminiscent of Oakeshott's conservative ideological stance.[15]

The most successful proponent of the end of ideology and indeed of history itself, is Francis Fukayama. His article 'The End of History?' published in the summer of 1989[16] aroused immediate and enormous controversy and was followed by a book entitled *The End of History and the Last Man* which elaborated on many of its themes.[17] In his article Fukayama argued that 'the unabashed victory of economic and political liberalism' over all competitors meant 'not just the end of the cold war, or the passing of a particular period of history, but the end of history as such: that is, the end-point of mankind's ideological evolution and the universalisation of Western liberal democracy as the final form of human government'.[18] Fukayama was not claiming that there would be no more events, but only that the final conceptual and political framework in which these events would take place had already been achieved. In the past, war had been a great catalyst of change: but to date there had been no example of liberal democratic states going to war with one another since, with the decline of ideology, the particular interests hitherto pursued by armed conflict could now be absorbed into the competitions of liberal capitalism. Nor did Fukayama see the persistence of poverty in Western societies as casting doubt on his thesis: poverty was due, not to market forces, but to cultural disadvantage which would eventually be eliminated in the face of the consumer abundance produced by modern capitalism. Moreover, Fukayama did not claim that the end of history yielded a perfect society – only that there was no prospect of a better alternative to liberal capitalism. Nationalism might flourish outside the most historically advanced countries of the world, but the large economic powers would conduct their rivalry in the future only by wars of trade. The revival of religious fundamentalism, too, was peripheral: it was only of real significance in Islam and even here limited to a relatively small area of the world. As for socialism, the only plausible variant left after the collapse of communism was the politics of social democracy which posed no threat to Fukayama's thesis since it fully accepted the primacy of market relations.

Fukayama's thesis was that there was an underlying evolutionary direction to history and that it arrived at an end state in which human nature's inbuilt struggle for individual recognition would at last be satisfied – and that the framework for this satisfaction was provided for in a liberal democratic and capitalist society. The form of this account is reminiscent of Marx's theory of history but the philosophical mentor of Fukayama is Marx's teacher Hegel. The philosophical background to which Fukayama appeals is Hegel's *Phenomenology* in the idiosyncratic interpretation given to it in Paris in the 1930s by the Russian emigré, Alexandre Kojève.[19] Central to Hegel's whole philosophy, according to Kojève, was the dialectic between master and slave: history continued in the past because the separation and struggle between masters who went to war and slaves who toiled precluded any mutual respect and recognition of individual work and dignity. With the spread of the principles of the French Revolution, however, universal equality was achieved. Each person received universal recognition 'as a Citizen enjoying all political rights and as a "juridical person" of the civil law' and 'desire thus being entirely satisfied, struggle and labour cease: history is over, there is nothing more *to do*'.[20] This absence of effort was not all to the good, however, and at the end of his article Fukayama painted a rather gloomy picture of the capitalist eternity he foresaw in which 'the end of history will be a very sad time. The struggle for recognition, the willingness to risk one's life for a purely abstract goal, the worldwide ideological struggle that called forth daring, courage, imagination and idealism, will be replaced by economic calculation, the endless solving of technical problems, environmental concerns, and satisfaction of sophisticated consumer demands. In the post-historical period there will be neither art nor philosophy, just the perpetual caretaking of the museum of the human spirit'.[21] The owl of Minerva did indeed paint grey on grey.

Thus Fukayama's position is a bit more ambivalent than his reputation as a bourgeois triumphalist might suggest. These ambiguities were strengthened in the three years that elapsed between his original article and its elaboration in book form. Here Fukayama provides an overall theory of history which stresses the role of science, unleased by capitalism, in the satisfying of human wants. He buttresses Hegel's account of the quest for existential recognition with a description of the spirited or wilful element in human nature drawn from Plato's *Republic*. This rather abstract and generalized philosophizing is supplemented by an extended and fluent account of the recent progress of democracy across the globe. The general message is still that 'if we are now at a point where we cannot imagine a world substantially different from our own, in which there is no apparent or obvious way in which the future will represent a fundamental improvement over our current order, then we must also take into consideration the possibility that History itself might be at an end'.[22] In the last section of his book, Fukayama turns to the second half of his title and imagines two criticisms from Left and Right to the effect that the very limited nature of human prospects that he describes does not allow for the most fundamental aspirations of human nature. From the Left comes the demand to extend human rights to promote a radical egalitarianism. Here Fukayama joins the recent backlash against 'political correctness' led by his teacher Alan Bloom.[23] It is, however, the challenge from the Right that Fukayama takes more seriously: that some will inevitably regard as shallow a society based solely on prosperity and efficiency and strive, not to be equal to others, but to be pre-eminent over them, thus subverting the very principles of liberal democracy. Fukayama is fairly optimistic about the capability of liberal democracy to cope with these criticisms, though the conclusion to his book does envisage the possibility of history's wagon train setting out on a new and more distant journey.[24] It is important to realize that on some crucial points Fukayama is deeply ambiguous. His strong historical metanarrative seems out of keeping with fashionable postmodernism but at the same time he endorses the directionless pluralism of contemporary society.[25] Further, as might be expected from anyone who tries to marry Plato to Hegel and their latter-day, if partial, disciples Strauss and Kojève, Fukayama sometimes retracts his confident assertion of the end of history. His readings of Plato and Hegel are, of course, extremely selective: for Plato, as his most articulate modern interpreter Simone Weil has shown, human achievement is due much more to self-transcendence than to self-aggrandizement. And central to Hegel's view of history is not struggle for recognition but progress in the consciousness of freedom.

Unsurprisingly, Fukayama's writing has generated a lot of controversy. Apart from the journalistic hype with which his first article was greeted, his ideas concentrate in an accessible form the enthusiasms and worries of the end of the twentieth century. Nevertheless his account does reveal serious gaps and weaknesses. It is surprising to find a complete neglect of Freud in a book which deals so extensively with the desires and motivations of the human mind. More importantly, Fukayama fails to engage seriously with either feminism – his individualistic description of the struggle for recognition is very male-orientated – or with ecological concerns – the global mass industrialization he envisages is likely to destroy the world's eco-system. In spite of the increasing gap between rich and poor nations, Fukayama is cavalierly confident about the stability and ever-widening appeal of liberal democracy. This confidence is based on the way in which he sees liberal democracy as bound up with capitalism. But this link is profoundly insecure since capitalism and democracy are very uneasy bedfellows. Capitalism is inevitably based on *some* form of exploitation and domination. As soon as democracy aspires to be more than a Schumpeterian competition among élites for the people's vote, it involves claims for equal economic entitlement and pressures which threaten the very inequalities on which capitalism depends. In other words 'capitalism as a system valorising motives of individual gain and self-realisation, and democratic citizenship as a source of social choice rooted in moral norms, point in different directions. There seems no reason to expect the hegemony of the first over the second to be a feature of all time'.[26] Indeed, Fukayama himself acknowledges this when he suggests that Western capitalism undermines any foundation of social solidarity and that if Asians appreciate the effect of corrosive individualism in Western societies, then 'a systematic illiberal and non-democratic alternative combining technocratic economic rationalism with paternalistic authoritarianism may gain ground in the Far East' and 'an overt rupture with democracy could occur in which the form itself would be rejected as a Western imposition, as irrelevant to the successful functioning of Asian societies as Western business management techniques are to their economies'.[27] Liberal democracy, with its self-destructive tendencies, would be just as doomed as Soviet communism and the end of history would be an East Asian Confucian capitalism with Lee Kuan Yew's Singapore as its model. Alternatively, if we take seriously the centrality accorded by Fukayama to Hegel's idea of the struggle for recognition, we might come to the conclusion that liberalism was seriously deficient. The criticism would be that 'the promise of universal, reciprocal recognition remains essentially unfulfilled in liberal societies: economic inequality brought about by capitalism *ipso facto* implies unequal recognition'.[28] The struggle, in other words, goes on until a radical egalitarianism, the only society which would ensure the full recognition of all, is achieved.[29] Either way, Fukayama's thesis of the end of history depends on that of Kojève and Kojève's claim that we are at the end of history 'stands or falls on the strength of the assertion that the recognition provided by contemporary liberal democratic states adequately satisfies the human desire for recognition'.[30] But if there is any validity in the above considerations, then the end of history, at least in Fukayama's sense, may yet by a very long way off.

Conclusion:
An End to Ideology
or Ideology
Without End?

As we have seen in the foregoing chapters, the discussion of ideology over the last two centuries has divided into two different approaches. In the first, the dominant contrast is between ideology and science. In the French rationalist tradition of de Tracy the application of reason to society would rid society of the irrational prejudices that had been so noxious in the past: the science of ideas (ideo-logy) would demystify society just as natural science had demystified nature. With a little help from Marx (and Napoleon), ideology then became associated with those ideas that were contrasted with science – as in the work of Durkheim or Althusser. The same science/ideology dichotomy is present in the strongly empiricist English-speaking tradition. The difference between the two lies in their opposing conceptions of what constitutes the science that excludes ideology: in the work of Althusser, for example, it is Marxism itself (and possibly psychoanalysis) which is that science. For Popper, on the other hand, both are the supreme examples of pseudo-Archimedian sciences. In the second tradition, often called historicist and associated with German writing, the search for a foothold has been strongly relativized. The problems of studying society were seen as radically different from those of studying nature. Ideology was connected with sectional interests, with social perspectives from which it was impossible completely to escape. Various more or less Olympian viewpoints were proposed in the shape of Hegel's Absolute Spirit, or Mannheim's free-floating intellectuals, or Habermas's ideal speech situation – but all as aspirations rather than realities.

One of the strengths of the Marxist tradition, which gave the concept of ideology the prominence that it now enjoys, lies in its catholic attitude to these two approaches. Both the science/ideology dichotomy and the connection of ideology with the social determination of ideas can be found in Marx himself. Both Engels and Althusser subscribe to the former, but they differ fundamentally in the importance they assign to ideology. It is clear, however, that the most fruitful Marxist contributions are those in the Germanic tradition. The relegation of ideology to the superstructure, whether in the scientific version of Engels or in the purely political one of Lenin, were dead ends. Marxism has indeed produced much banal talk about ideology: but it has also undoubted successes. Consider the sketchy though enormously insightful discussion by Gramsci in his *Prison Notebooks* of the incorporation of intellectuals by the medieval Church and the parallels he draws with the socialist movement; or the detailed analysis of the connections between Jansenist thought in the work of Pascal and Racine and the changing class structure of French society by Lukacs' pupil Lucien Goldmann. Both these studies retain the critical sense of ideology but without appealing either to a dubious concept of science or to a reductionist view of social processes.

It is in the empiricist tradition that the science/ideology dichotomy appears at its most vulnerable. A recent and well-informed commentary can still declare that those propounding an 'end of ideology' thesis in the United States are merely 'speaking in terms of, and reference to, empirical phenomena far removed from the methodological self-doubts – certainly justified – of the social sciences'.[1] This idea that the facts can speak for themselves has its origin in rather a different fact, namely that, in the words of the American historian Richard Hofstadter, 'It has been our fate as a nation not to have ideologies but to be one'.[2] The view of empiricists is that facts and values are separate at least in the sense that they can be separated in expressions where they are conjoined. But to say that facts (particularly social ones) are simply there, whereas values are the subject of free choice, is itself an evaluative view. Moreover, much recent work on ideology has linked it to the study of language and the symbols of everyday practical life where it is much less vulnerable to dismissal by reason or science than when it is simply treated as a systematic body of 'ideas'.

But if the science/ideology dichotomy will not do, nor will its opposite – the pale view of the omnipresence of ideology which has the additional, dangerous implication of reducing all social and political arguments to the status of mere propaganda. This can come in the form of an indiscriminating 'vulgar' Marxism to which virtually any aspect of contemporary society is a symptom of 'bourgeois' ideology. This approach neglects the vast amount of empirical evidence against the existence of any pervasive dominant ideology. The ideas of the ruling class do not permeate the whole of society: rather their role is assured by the fragmented nature of opposition to them. Nor is the ecumenical concept of ideology espoused by Martin Seliger in his *Ideology and Politics* more fruitful. For Seliger's definition of ideology, whereby it is any and every action-oriented set of beliefs organized into a coherent system, robs the concept of any critical edge. It also, in spite of vaunting its inclusive nature, restricts the definition to political belief-systems and thereby neglects the link between ideology and everyday life. Although the latter objection certainly does not apply to Clifford Geertz's view of 'ideology as a cultural system,'[3] his work, also, is overly benevolent to the concept of ideology. Since ideologies are, according to Geertz, 'most distinctively, maps of problematic social reality and matrices for the creation of collective conscience',[4] they are not, as ideologies, open to criticism.

The problem here is to avoid a circular vacuity. Daniel Bell, nostalgic for cold war certainties, has lamented that 'the concept of ideology has unravelled completely'.[5] He is right in that the demands of gender and race have been added to those of class to reveal the 'performative contradiction' of contemporary western societies: their principles of universal freedom and equality are constantly at odds with their own practices.[6] The arbitrary incoherence of much liberal thought has been powerfully exposed, from a different point of view, in the recent work of Alasdair MacIntyre.[7] But we do not need to accept the conservative conclusions that some have drawn nor give up completely on ideas of progress. Genuine emancipation can never be based on domination. The science/ideology dichotomy and the vulgar Marxist view share at least one redeeming feature in that they both attempt, however unsuccessfully, to link ideology to domination. For successful accounts of ideology must combine two attributes. The first, emphasized by Mannheim, is a hermeneutic subtlety which sees both that it is necessary to understand ideology before criticizing it and also adopts a self-reflexive attitude towards its own premises. The second, stressed in most strands of the Marxist tradition, is to preserve the concept's critical potential by linking it with analyses of control and domination, thereby extricating it from the labyrinth of relativism associated with the hermeneutic circle. Ideology may be 'an irretrievably fallen word'[8] – but then we live in a fallen society and, until we mend it, we will continue to be implicated in ideology. It follows that, although in principle there could be an end to ideology, it is certainly nowhere in sight – not even on the horizon. This is because ideology is best viewed not as a separate system of signs and symbols that could be contrasted with – and eventually replaced by – another, e.g. science of some sort. Ideology is rather an aspect of every system of signs and symbols in so far as they are implicated in an asymmetrical distribution of power and resources. And of which system is this not the case?

Notes

Chapter 1

1 On this idea, see the original article: W.B. Gallie, 'Essentially Contested Concepts' *Proceedings of the Aristotelian Society*, 1955–6, vol. 56, particularly pp. 171ff. On attempts to define ideology, see: R. Geuss, *The Idea of a Critical Theory*, Cambridge University Press, Cambridge, 1981, Pt I; M. Hamilton, 'The Elements of a Concept of Ideology', *Political Studies*, 1987, vol. 35, pp. 18ff; and T. Eagleton, *Ideology*, Verso, London, 1991, Ch. 1.

2 On ideology as no mere reflection but an active agent moulding the desires of those in its thrall, see: J. Elster, 'Belief, Bias and Ideology', in M. Hollis and S. Lukes, eds, *Rationality and Relativism*, Blackwell, Oxford, 1982.

3 J. Habermas, *Towards a Rational Society*, Heinemann, London, 1970, p. 99. For a similar view of the modernity of ideology see, for example, K. Mannheim, *Studies on the Left*, Routledge, London, 1952, p. 55 and M. Oakeshott, *Rationalism in Politics and Other Essays*, Methuen, London, 1962, p. 21.

4 See further on this the excellent article: B. Halpern, '"Myth" and "Ideology" in Modern Usage'. *History and Theory*, vol. 1, 1961, especially pp. 135ff.

5 See Ch. 7.

6 Baron d'Holbach. *The System of Nature* (translated by H.D. Robinson), Burt Franklin, New York, 1970, pp. viiiff.

7 K. Marx, *Selected Writings*, ed. D. McLellan, Oxford University Press, Oxford, 1977, p. 156.

8 Quoted in H. Barth, *Wahrheit und Ideologie*, Eugen Reutsch Verlag, Zurich and Stuttgart, 1961, p. 27.

9 The location of the 'Age' is a matter of dispute. Compare H.D. Aiken's *The Age of Ideology*, Mentor, New York, 1956, subtitled *The Nineteenth Century Philosophers* with K.D. Bracher's *The Age of Ideologies*, Weidenfeld, London, 1984, subtitled *A History of Political Thought in the Twentieth Century*.

10 See D. Coole, *Women in Political Theory*, Wheatsheaf, Brighton, 1988; S. Okin, *Gender, Justice and the Family*, Basic Books, New York, 1988; V. Bryson, *Feminist Political Thought*, Macmillan, Basingstoke, 1992.

11 See A. Dobson and P. Lucardie, *The Politics of Nature: Explorations in Green Political Theory*, Routledge, New York, 1993.

12 See particularly the trilogy by A. MacIntyre, *After Virtue*, 2nd edn, Duckworth, London, 1985; *Whose Justice? Which Rationality?*, University of Notre Dame Press, Notre Dame, 1988; *Three Rival Versions of Moral Enquiry*, University of Notre Dame Press, Notre Dame, 1990; and also the magisterial survey of the intellectual background to the moral dilemmas of the contemporary individual in C. Taylor, *Sources of the Self*, Cambridge University Press, Cambridge, 1985; and the useful collection of articles debating the issue in J. Horton and S. Mendus, *After MacIntyre*, Polity, Cambridge, 1994.

13 For an extreme example see the later work of J. Baudrillard in *Selected Writings*, ed. M. Poster, Polity, Cambridge, 1988.

Chapter 2

1 K. Marx, *Selected Writings*, ed. D. McLellan, Oxford University Press, Oxford, 1977, p. 64.

2 K. Marx, ibid. p. 164.

3 Ibid.

4 K. Marx, ibid. p. 169.

5 K. Marx, ibid., p. 176. For an argument that ruling ideas do not really rule subordinate groups in society but largely serve to give unity and direction to the ruling élite see: N. Abercrombie, S. Hill and Bill Turner, *The Dominant Ideology Thesis*, Allen and Unwin, London, 1980.

6 K. Marx, ibid., p. 164.

7 See J. Mepham, 'The Theory of Ideology in *Capital*', in *Issues in Marxist Philosophy*, eds J. Mepham and D.H. Ruben, Harvester, Brighton, 1979, pp. 143ff, and W. Mitchell, *Iconology: Image, Text, Ideology*, Chicago University Press, Chicago, 1986, Ch. 6.

8 K. Marx, op. cit., p. 436.

9 K. Marx, *Capital*, Lawrence and Wishart, London, 1972, vol. 3, p. 209.

10 For an elaboration of the contrast between 'lived' and 'intellectual' ideologies, see M. Billig, S. Condor, D. Edwards, M. Gane, D.

Middleton, A. Radley, *Ideological Dilemmas*, Sage, Beverly Hills, 1988 pp. 27ff.

11 K. Marx, *Selected Writings*, p. 455.

12 K. Marx, ibid., p. 164.

13 K. Marx, ibid., pp. 389f.

14 K. Marx, ibid., p. 172.

15 K. Marx, ibid., p. 389.

16 K. Marx, *Theories of Surplus Value*, Progress, Moscow, 1963, vol. 1, p. 285.

17 See especially, M. Seliger, *The Marxist Conception of Ideology*, Cambridge, 1977, pp. 28ff.

18 K. Marx, F. Engels, *Selected Correspondence*, Progress, Moscow, 1965, p. 459.

19 For an explicit rejection of the connection of ideology with false consciousness, see G. Therborn, *The Ideology of Power and the Power of Ideology*, Verso, London, 1980.

20 See further, W. Mitchell, *Iconology: Image, Text, Ideology*, University of Chicago Press, Chicago, 1986, Ch. 6; T. Eagleton, *Ideology*, Verso, London, 1991, pp. 70–80.

21 See L. Colletti, 'Marxism and the Dialectic', *New Left Review*, 1975, vol. 93.

22 B. Parekh, *Marx's Theory of Ideology*, Croom Helm, London, 1982, p. 219.

Chapter 3

1   K. Marx, F. Engels, *Selected Correspondence*, Foreign Languages Publishing House, Moscow, 1962. p. 467.

2   K. Marx, F. Engels, ibid., p. 423.

3   F. Engels, *Anti-Dühring*, Foreign Languages Publishing House, Moscow, 1971, p. 418.

4   F. Engels, ibid., p. 134.

5   F. Engels, ibid., p. 135.

6   F. Engels, *Ludwig Feuerbach*, Foreign Languages Publishing House, Moscow, 1968, p. 55.

7   K. Marx, F. Engels, *Selected Correspondence*, 1962, p. 459.

8   K. Marx, F. Engels, ibid., 1962, p. 455.

9   F. Engels, *Ludwig Feuerbach*, p. 55.

10 F. Engels, *Anti-Dühring*, Moscow, 1971, p. 135.

11 E. Bernstein, *Zur Geschichte und Theorie des Sozialismus*, Berlin, 1901, p. 282.

12 V. Lenin, *Selected Works*, Foreign Languages Publishing House, Moscow, 1963, vol. 1, pp. 156f.

13 V. Lenin, ibid., p. 149.

14 V. Lenin, ibid., p. 157.

15 G. Lukacs, *History and Class Consciousness*, Merlin Press, London, 1971, p. 224.

16 G. Lukacs, ibid., pp. 5ff.

17 G. Lukacs, ibid., pp. 258f.

18 G. Lukacs, ibid., p. 103.

19 G. Lukacs, ibid., p. 51. For a splendid example of Lukacs's method applied to literature and philosophy, see the study of the tragic world view of Pascal and Racine as expressive of the declining social power of their class in L. Goldman, *The Hidden God*, Routledge, London, 1955.

20 A. Gramsci, *Prison Notebooks*, ed. Q. Hoare and G. Nowell-Smith, Lawrence and Wishart, London, 1971.

21 A. Gramsci, ibid.

22 A. Gramsci, ibid., p. 377.

23 A. Gramsci, ibid., p. 326.

24 A. Gramsci, ibid., p. 60.

25 See R. Williams, *Marxism and Literature*, Oxford University Press, Oxford, 1977, Pt II Ch. 9 and also Ch. 6.

26 A. Gramsci, quoted in A. Davidson, *Antonio Gramsci*, Merlin, London, 1977, p. 260.

27 L. Althusser, *For Marx*, Allen Lane, London, 1969, p. 233.

28 L. Althusser, ibid., pp. 234f.

29 L. Althusser, *Lenin and Philosophy*, London, 1971, p. 160.

30 L. Althusser, ibid., p. 169.

31 L. Althusser, ibid., p. 152.

32 L. Althusser, *For Marx*, London, 1977, p. 232.

33 For an elaboration of this point, see W. Connolly, *Appearance and Reality in Politics*, Cambridge University Press, Cambridge, 1981, Ch. 2.

Chapter 4

1 Max Weber, 'Politics and Belief', *Gesammelte Politische Schriften*, Kaiser, Munich, 1921, p. 446.

2 Max Weber, *The Methodology of the Social Sciences*, Free Press, New York, 1946, p. 72.

3 E. Durkheim, *The Rules of Sociological Method*, ed. S. Lukes, Macmillan, London, 1982, p. 86.

4 E. Durkheim, ibid., p. 82.

5 S. Freud, *Totem and Taboo*, Penguin, Harmondsworth, 1939, p. 156.

6 S. Freud, *Group Psychology and the Analysis of the Ego*, Hogarth Press, London, 1967, p. 53.

7 S. Freud, ibid., p. 53.

8 S. Freud, *Totem and Taboo*, Harmondsworth, 1939, pp. 147f.

9 See, as a rather extreme example, L. Feuer, *Ideology and the Ideologists*, Blackwell, Oxford, 1975, particularly Ch. 4.

10 W. Reich, *The Mass Psychology of Fascism*, New York, 1970, p. 30.

11 W. Reich, ibid., p. 31.

12 M. Seliger, *Ideology and Politics*, Allen and Unwin, London, 1976, p. 13.

13 K. Mannheim, *Essays on the Sociology of Knowledge*, Routledge, London, 1957, pp. 90f.

14 K. Mannheim, *Ideology and Utopia*, Routledge and Kegan Paul, London, 1936, p. 51.

15 K. Mannheim, *Ideology and Utopia*, p. 66.

16 K. Mannheim, *Ideology and Utopia*, pp. 68f.

17 K. Mannheim. *Essays on the Sociology of Knowledge*, op. cit., p. 69.

18 K. Mannheim, ibid., p. 52.

19 cf. K. Mannheim, *Ideology and Utopia*, p. 239.

20 See particularly K. Mannheim, *Ideology and Utopia*, p. 239.

21 K. Mannheim, ibid., p. 239.

22 K. Mannheim, *Essays on the Sociology of Knowledge*, op. cit., p. 111.

23 K. Mannheim, ibid., p. 175.

24 cf. K. Mannheim, ibid., pp. 84ff.

25 K. Mannheim, ibid., p. 176.

26 K. Mannheim, *Ideology and Utopia*, p. 173.

27 K. Mannheim, *Essays on the Sociology of Knowledge*, op. cit., p. 239.

28 K. Mannheim, ibid., pp. 68f.

29 K. Mannheim, *Ideology and Utopia*, p. 270.

30 K. Mannheim, *Essays on the Sociology of Knowledge*, op. cit., p. 254.

31 K. Mannheim, ibid., p. 271.

32 K. Mannheim, ibid., p. 137.

33 K. Mannheim, *Ideology and Utopia*, p. 137.

34 K. Mannheim, *Essays on the Sociology of Knowledge*, op. cit., pp. 143f.

35 See A. Arblaster, 'Ideology and the Intellectuals', in R. Benewick, R. Berki, B. Parekh, *Knowledge and Belief in Politics*, Allen and Unwin, London, 1973, pp. 117ff.

36 cf. J. Gabel, 'Une pensée non-ideologique est-elle possible?' in *Sociologie de la Connaissance*, ed. J. Duvignaud, Sevil, Paris, 1979, pp. 17ff.

37 R. Merton, *Social Theory and Social Structure*, Free Press, Glencoe, New York, 1957, p. 503.

38 K. Mannheim, *Ideology and Utopia*, p. 259.

39 M. Cranston, 'Ideology and Mr. Lichtheim', *Encounter*, vol. 31, 1968.

40 J. LaPalombara, 'Decline of Ideology: A Dissent and an Interpretation', *American Political Science Review*, vol. 60, 1966, p. 13.

Chapter 5

1 See G. Sartori, 'Politics, Ideology and Belief Systems', *American Political Science Review* no. 3, 1969, p. 398.

2 Ibid., pp. 5f.

3 K. Mannheim, *Ideology and Utopia*, p. 230.

4 K. Mannheim, ibid., p. 236.

5 R. Aron, *Opium of the Intellectuals*, Norton, New York, 1962, p. 314.

6 S. Lipset, *Political Man*, Heinemann, London, 1960, p. 408.

7 D. Bell, *The End of Ideology*, Free Press, Glencoe, New York, 1960 p. 370.

8 In a recent defence of his avowedly normative definition, Bell still claims that 'ideology deals with social movements that seek to mobilize men for the realization of eschatological creeds in secular terms, and in this fusion of political formulas and passions, ideology provides a faith and a set of moral certitudes by which ends are used to justify immoral means'. See D. Bell 'The End of Ideology Revisited', Pt I, *Government and Opposition*, vol. 23, 1988.

9 M. Oakeshott, *Rationalism in Politics and Other Essays*, Methuen, London, 1962, p. 22. For a useful account of Oakeshott and his school, see H. Williams, *The Concept of Ideology*, Harvester, Brighton, 1989, Ch. 3.

10 K. Minogue, *Alien Powers: The Pure Theory of Ideology*, Weidenfeld and Nicholson, London, 1985, p. 4, and K. Minogue 'Ideology after the Collapse of Communism', in *The End of 'Isms'? Reflections on the Fate of Ideological Politics after Communism's Collapse*, ed. A. Shtromas, Blackwell, Oxford, 1994, p. 17. See also W. Greenleaf, *The British Political Tradition: the Ideological Heritage*, Methuen, London, 1983, vol. 2 and the criticism of this view in A. Vincent, 'British Conservatism and the Problem of Ideology', in *Political Studies*, vol. 42, June 1994.

11 B. Crick, *In Defence of Politics*, Penguin, Harmondsworth, 1964, p. 34.

12 See also the contributions to *Totalitarianism* ed. C.J. Friedrich, Harvard University Press, Cambridge, Mass. 1954.

13 H. Arendt, *The Origins of Totalitarianism*, Harcourt Brace, New York, 1973, p. 471.

14 H. Arendt, op. cit., p. 469.

15 E. Shils, 'The Concept and Function of Ideology', *International Encyclopaedia of the Social Sciences*, vol. VII, 1968, p. 74.

16 H. Johnson, 'Ideology and the Social System', op. cit. p. 77.

17 See K. Popper, *The Open Society and Its Enemies*, Routledge, London, 1952.

18 H. Marcuse, *Negations*, Penguin, Harmondsworth, 1972, pp. 223f.

19 G. Sartori, 'Politics Ideology and Belief Systems,' *American Political Science Review*, vol. 63, 1969, p. 403.

20 G. Sartori, ibid., p. 406.

21 G. Sartori, ibid., p. 411.

22 G. Sartori, ibid.

23 G. Sartori, ibid., p. 401.

24 G. Sartori, ibid., p. 402.

25 W. Mullins, 'On the Concept of Ideology in Political Science', *American Political Science Review*, vol. 66, 1972, pp. 509f.

26 G. Sartori, op. cit., p. 407.

27 G. Sartori, ibid.

28 G. Sartori, ibid., p. 410.

29 R. Dahl, *A Preface to Democratic Theory*, Chicago University Press, Chicago, 1956, p. 132.

30 R. Dahl, ibid., p. 132.

31 R. Dahl, ibid.

32 S. Lukes, *Power: A Radical Analysis*, Macmillan, London, 1974, p. 23.

33 R. Dahl, *Who Governs?* Yale University Press, New Haven, 1961. See, however, the evolution of Dahl's views in R. Dahl, *A Preface to Economic Democracy*, Yale University Press, New Haven, 1984, for a sharp re-thinking of property rights.

34 On the difficulties inherent in the concept of 'interests', see further W. Connolly, *The Terms of Political Discourse*, Martin Robertson, London, 1983, pp. 45ff.

35 P. Bachrach, *The Theory of Democratic Elitism*, University Press of America, Washington DC, 1980, pp. 83f.

Chapter 6

1 M. Horkheimer, *Critical Theory*, Herder and Herder, New York, 1972, p. 8.

2 H. Marcuse, *One-Dimensional Man*, Routledge and Kegan Paul, London, 1964, pp. 105f.

3 T. Kuhn, *The Structure of Scientific Revolutions*, Chicago, 1973, p. viii.

4 For a nuanced statement of this point of view with regard to ideology, see P. Ricoeur, *Hermeneutics and the Human Sciences*, ed. J. Thompson, Cambridge University Press, Cambridge, 1984, pp. 232ff.

5 C. Levi-Strauss, *The Savage Mind*, Chicago, Chicago University Press, 1966, p. 269.

6 C. Levi-Strauss, *The Raw and the Cooked*, Cape, London, 1970, p. 12.

7 R. Barthes, *Mythologies*, Paladin, London, 1973, p. 32. For an extended demonstration of how the media exposure of the British royal family affirms their regal image, see M. Billig, *Talking of the Royal Family*, Routledge, London, 1992.

8 K. Marx and F. Engels, *The German Ideology, Collected Works*, vol. 5, Lawrence and Wishart, London, p. 44.

9 G. Kress and R. Hodge, *Language as Ideology*, Routledge, London, 1979, p. 9. See also the later writings of Pierre Bourdieu which contain micro-sociological accounts of how the 'symbolic violence' of contemporary society regulates our actions in accordance with unconscious norms and excludes and silences those who cannot compete.

10 G. Kress and R. Hodge, ibid., p. 10.
11 The classic work on this is J.L. Austin, *How to do Things with Words*, ed. J.O. Urmson and M. Sbisa, Clarendon Press, Oxford, 1962, pp. 4ff. On the politics of discourse analysis, see S. Hall and M. Jaques, *New Times: The Changing Face of Politics in the 1990s*, Lawrence and Wishart, London, 1989.
12 E. Leach, *Political Systems of Highland Burma*, Bell, London, 1954, p. 278.
13 cf. N. Abercrombie, S. Hill, D. Turner, *The Dominant Ideology Thesis*, Allen and Unwin, London, 1980, pp. 59ff.
14 J. Habermas, *Theory and Practice*, Heinemann, London, 1971, p. 169.
15 J. Habermas, ibid.
16 J. Habermas, *Legitimation Crisis*, Heinemann, London, 1976, p. 93.
17 J. Habermas, *Logik der Sozialwissenschaften*, Frankfurt, 1970, quoted by T. McCarthy in 'Introduction' to *Legitimation Crisis*, London, 1976, p. xiii.
18 J. Habermas, 'Summation and Response', *Continuum* vol. 8, 1970, p. 129.
19 Quoted by T. McCarthy, 'A Theory of Communicative Competence', *Philosophy of Social Science*, vol. 3, 1973, p. 140.
20 J. Habermas, *Legitimation Crisis*, London, 1976, p. 113.
21 J. Habermas, *Knowledge and Human Interests*, Heinemann, London, 1978, p. 314.

Chapter 7

1 For a careful discussion see M. Rose, *The Post-modern and the Post-industrial*, Cambridge University Press, Cambridge, 1992, Ch. 1.
2 A. Heller and F. Feher, *The Postmodern Political Condition*, Polity, Cambridge, p. 11.
3 See P. Kamuf, *A Derrida Reader*, Columbia University Press, New York, 1991, Part 1; and R. Gaschè, *The Turn of the Mirror: Derrida and the Philosophy of Reflection*, Harvard University Press, Cambridge, Mass., Ch. 8.
4 F. Jameson, *Postmodernism, or, The Culture Logic of Late Capitalism*, Verso, London, 1991, p. 277.
5 This is the last sentence of M. Foucault's *The Order of Things*, Tavistock, London, 1970.
6 K. Marx and F. Engels, *The Communist Manifesto*, Oxford University Press, Oxford, p. 6.
7 F. Jameson, op. cit., p. 4.
8 See here particularly D. Harvey, *The Condition of Postmodernity*, Blackwell, Oxford, 1990, Pts III and IV.

9 See particularly V. Perez-Diaz, *The Return of Civil Society*, Harvard University Press, London, 1993, Ch. 2. Civil Society has been celebrated from the Right by such writers as Gray and Oakeshott and from the Left by Keane and most recently by J. Cohen and A. Arato in *Civil Society and Political Theory*, MIT Press, Cambridge, Mass., 1992, with its postmodern apogee being reached in E. Laclau and C. Mouffe, *Hegemony and Socialist Strategy*, Verso, London, 1985.

10 See T. Eagleton, *Ideology*, Verso, London, 1991, p. 165.

11 cf. J. Habermas, *The Philosophical Discourse of Modernity: Twelve Lectures*, MIT Press, Cambridge, Mass., 1977.

12 F. Jameson, op. cit., p. 1. See also, more explicitly, p. 263; T. Eagleton, op. cit., p. xii; and J. Derrida, 'A Lecture on Marx', *New Left Review*, vol. 205, 1994, pp. 49ff.

13 R. Rorty, *Contingency, Irony, and Solidarity*, Cambridge University Press, Cambridge, 1989, p. 63.

14 R. Rorty, 'The Priority of Democracy to Philosophy', in R. Vaughan, ed., *The Virginia Statute of Religious Freedom*, University of Wisconsin Press, Madison, 1988, p. 264.

15 Ibid., p. 53.

16 F. Fukayama, 'The End of History?', *The National Interest*, vol. 16, Summer, 1989.

17 F. Fukayama, *The End of History and the Last Man*, The Free Press, New York, 1992.

18 F. Fukayama, 'The End of History?', pp. 3f.

19 See A. Kojève, *Introduction to the Reading of Hegel*, Basic Books, New York, 1969.

20 A. Kojève, ibid., p. 237.

21 F. Fukayama, 'The End of History?', p. 18.

22 F. Fukayama, *The End of History and the Last Man*, p. 51.

23 See A. Bloom, *The Closing of the American Mind*, Simon and Schuster, New York, 1987.

24 cf. F. Fukayama, *The End of History and the Last Man*, p. 339.

25 See Kojève, op. cit., p. 238 on the disappearance of 'man' and the advent of an animal society driven solely by the mindless merry-go-round of pleasure and play.

26 M. Rustin, 'No Exit from Capitalism?', *New Left Review*, vol. 193, 1992, p. 107.

27 F. Fukayama, *The End of History and the Last Man*, p. 243.

28 Ibid., p. 289.

29 See further the excellent article by J. McCarney, 'Shaping Ends: Reflections on Fukayama', *New Left Review*, vol. 202, 1993.

30 J. McCarney, ibid., p. 207.

Chapter 8

1 W. Carlsnaes, *The Concept of Ideology and Political Analysis*, Greenwood Press, Westport, 1981, p. 238.

2 Quoted in S.P. Huntington, *American Politics: The Promise of Disharmony*, Belknap Press, New York, 1981, p. 25.

3 See Geertz's influential article 'Ideology as a Cultural System' in *Ideology and Discontent*, ed. D. Apter, Free Press, New York, 1964.

4 C. Geertz, ibid., p. 64.

5 D. Bell, 'The End of Ideology Revisited', Pt II, *Government and Opposition*, 1988, p. 321.

6 See the sharp exposition in D. Turner, *Marxism and Christianity*, Blackwell, Oxford, 1983, Ch. 3.

7 See J. Horton and S. Mendus, *After MacIntyre: Critical Perspectives on the Work of Alasdair MacIntyre*, Polity, Cambridge, 1994, particularly Chs 1, 13, and 14.

8 D. Bell, op cit., p. 331.

Further Reading

Chapter 1

On the origins of the concept of ideology, see Ch. 1 of Hans Barth's *Truth and Ideology*. There are shorter accounts in Seliger's *The Marxist Conception of Ideology*, Lichtheim's *The Concept of Ideology*, pp. 12ff, and Bendix's article, 'The Age of Ideology: Persistent and Changing', pp. 296ff. For the French *ideologues*, see particularly Cheryl Welch's *Liberty and Utility* and the two books on Destutt de Tracy by Kennedy and Head.

A virtually exhaustive account of the manifold senses of the concept is given in Arne Naess *et al.*, *Democracy, Ideology and Objectivity*, pp. 143ff. There is a shorter version in Robert Lane's 'The Meanings of Ideology'. See also Geuss's *Idea of a Critical Theory*, Ch. 1, Eagleton's *Ideology*, Ch. 1, and Hamilton's article 'The Elements of the Concept of Ideology'.

Attempts to distinguish ideology from the related concepts of myth and utopia can be found in the following articles: Lee McDonald, 'Myth, Politics and Political Science'; Ben Halpern, ' "Myth" and "Ideology" in Modern Usage'; and Willard Mullins, 'On the Concept of Ideology in Political Science'.

For Michael Oakeshott's strictures on ideology, see the title essay of his *Rationalism in Politics*. This approach is carried out in more detail in a collection by Oakeshott's disciples: David Manning, ed., *The Form of Ideology*. For the same scepticism about received thinking on ideology see Kenneth Minogue's recent lively polemic, *Alien Powers: The Pure Theory of Ideology*. For a good commentary on the Oakeshottian view of ideology, see Williams's *Concepts of Ideology*, Ch. 3.

Among more general works on ideology, Norman Birnbaum's 'The Sociological Study of Ideology 1940–1960', is immensely useful, though necessarily chronologically confined. Perhaps the best book is Jorge

Larrain's *The Concept of Ideology*, written from a mildly Marxist viewpoint. John Plamenatz's *Ideology* combines rather uneasily the historical and the analytic. Always stimulating is Alvin Gouldner's disorganized *Dialectics of Ideology and Technology*. Martin Seliger's *Ideology and Politics* pursues the theme of an inclusive conception of ideology through virtually all the recent literature. Two short treatments which deal knowledgeably and clearly with the more 'continental' aspects of recent discussion are Anthony Giddens, *Central Problems in Social Theory*, Ch. 5, and Stuart Hall's 'The Hinterland of Science: Ideology and the "Society of Knowledge"'. Boudon's *The Analysis of Ideology* usefully blends continental European and Anglo-Saxon approaches, while Eagleton's *Ideology*, witty, powerful, neo-Marxist, is highly recommended.

Chapter 2

A book-length treatment is available in Bhikhu Parekh's *Marx's Theory of Ideology*, which is a good exposition with sensible criticisms. See also Larrain's two books: Ch. 1 of *The Concept of Ideology* and Ch. 2 of *Marxism and Ideology*, which are sound and thoughtful, though over-protective of Marx. Seliger's critique in *The Marxist Conception of Ideology* suffers from an over-hasty identification of Marx's concept with that of 'false-consciousness'. The same is true of Ch. 2 of Carlsnaes's *The Concept of Ideology and Political Analysis*, which is the best example of a critique of Marx from a positivist/analytical viewpoint. But see also, in the same vein, Ch. 3 of Plamenatz's *Ideology*. A very sharp account of Marx which tries forlornly to harmonize his conception with that of Lenin is Ch. 1 of McCarney's *The Real World of Ideology*. Mepham's 'The Theory of Ideology in *Capital*' stresses the differences between *Capital* and *The German Ideology*. On the former see Geras's article 'Marx and the Critique of Political Economy' and on the latter Mitchell's *Iconology*, Ch. 6. For brief treatments sympathetic to Marx see Hans Barth, *Truth and Ideology*, Ch. 3; John McMurtry, *The Structure of Marx's World View*, Ch. 5 and Cohen's *Karl Marx's Theory of History*, Ch. 5. A fascinating attempt to reconstruct Marx's theory on the basis of methodological individualism is to be found in Jon Elster, *Making Sense of Marx*, Ch. 8. See also Jakubowski's *Ideology and Superstructure*, Williams's *Concepts of Ideology*, Ch. 1, Peffer's *Marxism, Morality and Social Justice*, Ch. 6 and Eagleton's *Ideology*, Ch. 2.

Chapter 3

General background to this chapter can be found in Jordan's *The Evolution of Dialetical Materialism* and McLellan's *Marxism After Marx*. See also the huge though patchy collection by Nelson and Grossburg, *Marxism and the Interpretation of Culture*.

For the view that there is more to Engels on this subject than had previously been thought, see Balibar's *Masses, Classes, Ideas*, Chs. 4 and 6. Lenin's most accessible work in which there is reference to ideology is *What is to be done?*, available in most collections. An excellent general treatment of Lenin is Harding's *Lenin's Political Thought*. His views on ideology are given sympathetic treatment in Ch. 2 of Larrain's *Marxism and Ideology* and even more so in Ch. 2 of McCarney's *The Real World of Ideology*; a fuller exposition and criticism is to be found in Ch. 3 of Carlsnaes's *The Concept of Ideology and Political Analysis*.

For Lukacs's more philosophically oriented version of Lenin, see his *History and Class Consciousness*, paticularly the three central essays on class consciousness, reification and historical materialism. There is commentary, again, in Ch. 2 of Larrain's *Marxism and Ideology*, and in Ch. 2 of McCarney's *The Real World of Ideology*; also in Roizin McDonagh's 'Ideology and False Consciousness: Lukacs', also in Eagleton, Ch. 4 and Perkins's *Marxism and the Proletariat*, Chs 5 and 6. For a more hostile treatment, see Martin Seliger, *The Marxist Conception of Ideology*, especially Ch. 4.

Gramsci's remarks on ideology are to be found scattered throughout his *Prison Notebooks*, especially in the sections entitled 'The State and Civil Society' and 'Problems of Philosophy and History'. There is thorough discussion in Chantal Mouffe, 'Hegemony and Ideology in Gramsci'. See also Stuart Hall *et al.*, 'Politics and Ideology: Gramsci', and Ch. 3 of Larrain's *Marxism and Ideology*. For a thoroughly post-modern reading, see Renate Holub's *Antonio Gramsci*.

Finally, Althusser's conception of ideology can be found most easily in his essay in 'Ideology and Ideological State Apparatuses', though *For Marx, Reading Capital*, and *Essays in Self-Criticism* should also be consulted. Two accessible commentaries are Gregor McLennan's 'Althusser's Theory of Ideology' and Paul Hirst's article of the same title. For a recent attempt to think about ideology in an Althusserian mode, see Therborn's *The Ideology of Power and The Power of Ideology*. See also the excellent books by Benton and Elliott, the two readers edited by Kaplan and Sprinkler and by Elliott, and the careful commentary in Ricoeur's *Lectures on Ideology and Utopia*, Chs 7, 8 and 9.

Chapter 4

The contributions of Durkheim and Weber are very briefly discussed in Bendix's article 'The Age of Ideology: Persistent and Changing'. Durkheim's explicit references to ideology are mostly in his *Rules of Sociological Method*, though a different approach seems to be implicit in his *Elementary*

Forms of the Religious Life. There is a clear account at the end of Ch. 3 of Larrain's *The Concept of Ideology*. See also Turner's collection *Emile Durkheim: Sociologist and Moralist*, Part I. Weber has no concept of ideology as such, but see his *The Protestant Ethic and the Spirit of Capitalism*, together with Gidden's introduction for his general approach, and the concise commentary provided by Frank Parkin's *Weber*, especially Ch. 2, also Ricoeur's *Lectures on Ideology and Utopia*, Chs 11 and 12, and Turner's *Max Weber: From History to Modernity*.

The main works of Freud of interest here are *Totem and Taboo*, *The Future of an Illusion*, and *Civilization and its Discontents*. See further Larrain's *The Concept of Ideology*, Ch. 3, the general comments by Roazen in *Freud: Social and Political Thought*, especially Ch. 4 and the collections by Neu, *The Cambridge Companion to Freud*, particularly the contributions by Paul and Deigh, and by Spurling, *Sigmund Freud: Critical Assessments*, Parts I and II. The relevant works of Reich and Pareto are in the bibliography.

Mannheim's classic work on the subject is *Ideology and Utopia*. See also the collection *From Karl Mannheim*, with a useful introduction by Kurt Wolff. David Kettler's *Mannheim* is a good short introduction. Post-war interest in Mannheim was given impetus by Merton's *Social Theory and Social Structure*, Ch. 13. Expositions and criticisms of Mannheim are to be found in Larrain's *The Concept of Ideology*, Ch. 4 and Carlsnaes's *The Concept of Ideology and Political Analysis*, Ch. 4. The subtlest and best discussion is in Simonds's *Karl Mannheim's Sociology of Knowledge*. See also Remmling, *The Sociology of Karl Mannheim*, Loaders's *The Intellectual Development of Karl Mannheim*, and Williams, *Concepts of Ideology*, Ch. 2.

Chapter 5

Two short and influential summaries of the mainstream conception of ideology in the United States are available in the articles by Edward Shils 'The Concept and Function of Ideology' and Harry Johnson, 'Ideology and the Social System'. Sartori's 'Politics, Ideology and Belief Systems' is an unabashed attempt to put such conceptions to work. For more would-be empirical discussions of ideology, see Robert Lane, *Political Ideology*, and the articles by Robert Putnam, 'Studying Elite Political Culture: The Case of Ideology' and by Philip Converse, 'The Nature of Belief Systems in Mass Publics'. A conceptually more subtle approach can be found in two contributions from Willard Mullins: 'On the Concept of Ideology in Political Science' and 'Sartori's Concept of Ideology: A Dissent and an Alternative'. A more basic critique of this whole approach is in William Connolly's book *Political Science and Ideology* and in Charles Taylor's article 'Neutrality in Political Science'.

The connection between a certain concept of ideology and 'totalitarianism' is spelt out in Friedrich and Brzezinski, *Totalitarian Dictatorship and Autocracy*, the last two chapters of Hannah Arendt's *The Origins of Totalitarianism*, and Hansen's *Hannah Arendt*.

The two main exponents of an end of ideology thesis are Daniel Bell, *The End of Ideology*, and Seymour Lipset, in the last chapter of *Political Man*. Further contributions and criticism are available in Chaim Waxman's collection, *The End of Ideology Debate*. See also Bell's reprise in his two 1988 articles and the reading referred to under Ch. 7. For a view that the old enemy is renascent under the bizarre description of political correctness see Bloom, *The Closing of the American Mind*, and D'Souza *Illiberal Education*. For good surveys, see Hoeveler's *Watch on the Right*, Himmelstein's *To the Right* and Faulkner's contribution to the Shtromas collection *The End of Isms?*

Chapter 6

For the attack on the modern applications of science through technology, see Horkheimer and Adorno, *Dialectic of the Enlightenment*, and Marcuse, *One-Dimensional Man*, particularly Ch. 6. A questioning of the objectivity of natural science itself is to be found in Thomas Kuhn's *The Structure of Scientific Revolutions* and, in a more extreme form, in Paul Feyerabend's *Against Method*.

Two classics of the structuralist approach to ideology are Roland Barthes, *Mythologies*, and (more difficult) Levi-Strauss, *The Savage Mind*. A good general introduction to structuralist thought is John Sturrock's *Structuralism and Since*. A more specific discussion is in Ch. 5 of Larrain's *The Concept of Ideology*. Accessible introductions to Levi-Strauss are Leach's *Levi-Strauss* and Badcock's *Levi-Strauss: Structuralism and Sociological Theory*. Marxist attempts to assimilate this line of thought can be found in the works of Louis Althusser and its effluents discussed in Ch. 3 above.

For more strictly linguistic discussions of ideology of structuralist inspiration, see Robert Fowler *et al. Language and Control*, Kress and Hodge, *Language and Ideology*, and Lee's *Competing Discourses*. An excellent discussion of this whole difficult area is John Thompson's *Studies in the Theory of Ideology*. See also the sharp and uncompromising account in Part I of Denys Turner's *Marxism and Christianity*.

For Habermas, see his various works listed in the bibliography below. Good commentaries are David Held, *Introduction to Critical Theory*, Chs 9–11; David Held and John Thompson, eds, *Habermas: Critical Debates*; and Alvin Gouldner, *The Dialectic of Ideology and Technology*, Chs 11 and 12. See also the careful discussion in Geuss, *The Idea of a Critical Theory* and White, *The Recent Work of Jürgen Habermas*.

Chapter 7

The classic here is Lyotard's *The Postmodern Condition* on which see Drolet's article on 'Lyotard's Post-Modern Politics'. See also the Derrida reader by Kamuf. For a favourable account from the Left, see Jameson's magisterial *Postmodernism*; for a hostile account, equally from the Left, see Harvey's coruscating *The Condition of Postmodernity*. The two most accessible introductions are Margaret Rose's *The Post-modern and the Post-industrial* and Stephen White's *Political Theory and Postmodernism*. There is also a good discussion in Heller and Feher's *The Postmodern Political Condition* and in Wagner's *A Sociology of Modernity*, Parts IV and V.

For Rorty, see his *Contingency, Irony and Solidarity*, and the discussions in Bernstein, Chs 8 and 9 and in Malachowski's collection *Reading Rorty*, Parts IV and V.

On Fukayama, see the articles by Halliday and Rustin. Also the excellent discussions in McCarney's 'Shaping Ends' and Anderson's *A Zone of Engagement*, Ch. 13.

Bibliography

Abercrombie, N., Hill, S. and Turner, B., *The Dominant Ideology Thesis*, Allen and Unwin, London, 1980.

Aiken, H., *The Age of Ideology*, Mentor, New York, 1956.

Althusser, L., *For Marx*, Allen Lane, London, 1969.

Althusser, L., 'Ideology and Ideological State Apparatuses', in *Lenin and Philosophy*, New Left Books, London, 1971.

Althusser, L., *Essays in Self-Criticism*, New Left Books, London, 1976.

Althusser, L., and Balibar, E. *Reading Capital*, New Left Books, London, 1970.

Anderson, P., *A Zone of Engagement*, Verso, London, 1992.

Ansell-Pearson, K., *Nietzsche contra Rousseau: A Study of Nietzsche's Moral and Political Thought*, Cambridge University Press, New York, 1991.

Arblaster, A., 'Ideology and the Intellectuals', in *Knowledge and Belief in Politics*, ed. R. Benewick, R. Berki, B. Parekh, Allen and Unwin, London, 1973.

Arendt, H., *The Origins of Totalitarianism*, Harcourt, Brace, Jovanovich, New York, 1973.

Aron, R., *The Opium of the Intellectuals*, Norton, New York, 1962.

Bachrach, P., *The Theory of Democratic Elitism: A Critique*, University Press of America, Lanham, 1980.

Badcock, J., *Levi-Strauss: Structuralism and Sociological Theory*, Hutchinson, London, 1975.

Balibar, E., *Masses, Classes, Ideas: Studies on Politics and Philosophy Before and After Marx*, Routledge, New York, 1994.

Barth, H., *Truth and Ideology*, University of California Press, Los Angeles, 1977.

Barthes, R., *Mythologies*, Paladin Books, London, 1973.

Bauman, Z., *Intimations of Postmodernity*, Routledge, New York, 1992.

Bell, D., *The End of Ideology – On the Exhaustion of Political Ideas in the Fifties*, Free Press of Glencoe, New York, 1960.

Bell, D., 'The End of Ideology Revisited', Parts I and II, *Government and Opposition*, vol. 23, 1988.

Bendix, R., 'The Age of Ideology: Persistent and Changing', in *Ideology and Discontent*, ed. D. Apter, Free Press, Glencoe, New York, 1964.

Benton, T., *The Rise and Fall of Structural Marxism: Althusser and His Influence*, Macmillan, London, 1984.

Bernstein, R., *The New Constellation: The Ethical Political Horizons of Modernity/Postmodernity*, Polity, Cambridge, 1991.

Billig, M., Condor, S., Edwards, D., Gane, M., Middleton, D., Radley, A., *Ideological Dilemmas: A Social Psychology of Everyday Thinking*, Sage, Beverly Hills, 1988.

Birnbaum, N., 'The Sociological Study of Ideology 1940–1960, A Trend Report and Bibliography', *Current Sociology*, vol. 9, 1960.

Bloom, A., *The Closing of the American Mind*, Simon and Schuster, New York, 1987.

Boudon, R., *The Analysis of Ideology*, Polity, Cambridge, 1989.

Bourdieu, P., *Outline of a Theory of Practice*, Cambridge University Press, Cambridge, 1977.

Bracher, K., *The Age of Ideologies: A History of Political Thought in the Twentieth Century*, Weidenfeld, London, 1984.

Carlsnaes, W., *The Concept of Ideology and Political Analysis*, Greenwood Press, Westport, 1981.

Cohen, G., *Karl Marx's Theory of History: A Defence*, Clarendon Press, Oxford, 1978.

Cohen, J. and Arato, A., *Civil Society and Political Theory*, MIT Press, Cambridge, 1992.

Colletti, L., 'Marxism and the Dialectic', *New Left Review*, vol. 93, 1975.

Connolly, W., *Political Science and Ideology*, Atherton Press, New York, 1967.

Connolly, W., *Appearance and Reality in Politics*, Cambridge University Press, Cambridge, 1981.

Converse, P., 'The Nature of Belief Systems in Mass Publics', in *Ideology and Discontent*, ed. D. Apter, Free Press, Glencoe, New York, 1964.

Crick, B., *In Defence of Politics*, Penguin, Harmondsworth, 1964.

Dahl, R., *A Preface to Democratic Theory*, Chicago University Press, Chicago, 1956.

Dahl, R., *Who Governs?*, Yale University Press, New Haven, 1961.

Derrida, J., *Spectres of Marx: The State of the Debt, the Work of Mourning, and the New International*, Routledge, New York, 1995.

Dobson, A. and Lucardie, P., *The Politics of Nature: Explorations in Green Political Theory*, Routledge, New York, 1993.

Drolet, M., 'The Wild and the Sublime: Lyotard's Post-Modern Politics', *Political Studies*, vol. 42, 1994.

D'Souza, D., *Illiberal Education: The Politics of Sex, Race and Gender on Campus*, The Free Press, New York, 1991.

Duncan, G., 'Understanding Ideology', *Political Studies*, vol. 35, 1987.

Durkheim, E., *Elementary Forms of the Religious Life*, 2nd edn, Allen and Unwin, London, 1976.

Durkheim, E., *Rules of Sociological Method*, and Selected Texts on Society and its Method, ed., S. Lukes, Macmillan, London, 1982.

Eagleton, T., *Ideology: An Introduction*, Verso, London, 1991.

Eatwell, R., and Wright, A. *Contemporary Political Ideologies*, Pinter, London, 1993.

Elliott, G., *Althusser: The Detour of Theory*, Verso, London, 1987.

Elliott, G., ed., *Althusser: A Critical Reader*, Blackwell, Oxford, 1994.

Elster, J., 'Beliefs, Bias and Ideology' in *Rationality and Relativism*, eds M. Hollis and S. Lukes, Blackwell, Oxford, 1982.

Elster, J., *Making Sense of Marx*, Cambridge University Press, Cambridge, 1985.

Engels, F., *Anti-Duhring*, Foreign Languages Publishing House, Moscow, 1971.

Feuer, L., *Ideology and the Ideologists*, Blackwell, Oxford, 1975.

Feyerabend, P., *Against Method*, New Left Books, London, 1975.

Fish, S., *There's No Such Thing as Free Speech, and It's a Good Thing, Too*, Oxford University Press, New York, 1994.

Fowler, R., *Language and Control*, Routledge and Kegan Paul, London, 1979.

Freud, S., *The Future of an Illusion*, Hogarth Press, London, 1928.

Freud, S., *Totem and Taboo*, Penguin, Harmondsworth, 1938.

Freud, S., *Civilization and its Discontents*, Norton, New York, 1951.

Freud, S., *Group-Psychology and the Analysis of the Ego*, Hogarth Press, London, 1967.

Friedrich, C., and Brzezinski, Z., *Totalitarian Dictatorship and Autocracy*, 2nd edn, Harvard University Press, Cambridge, 1965.

Fukayama, F., *The End of History and the Last Man*, The Free Press, New York, 1992.

Gallie, W., 'Essentially Contested Concepts', *Proceedings of the Aristotelian Society*, vol. 56. 1955–6.

Geras, N., 'Marx and the Critique of Political Economy' in *Ideology in the Social Sciences*, ed. R. Blackburn, Fontana, London, 1972.

Geuss, R., *The Idea of a Critical Theory*, Cambridge University Press, Cambridge, 1981.

Giddens, A., *Central Problems in Social Theory*, Macmillan, London, 1979.

Goldstein, J., ed., *Foucault and the Writing of History*, Blackwell, Oxford, 1994.

Gouldner, A., *Dialectic of Ideology and Technology*, Macmillan, London, 1976.

Gramsci, A., *Selections from the Prison Notebooks*, eds Q. Hoare and G. Nowell-Smith, Lawrence and Wishart, London, 1971.

Gutting, G., *Michel Foucault's Archaeology of Scientific Reason*, Cambridge University Press, Cambridge, 1989.

Habermas, J., *Towards a Rational Society*, Heinemann, London, 1970.

Habermas, J., *Theory and Practice*, Heinemann, London, 1971.

Habermas, J., *Legitimation Crisis*, Heinemann, London, 1976.

Habermas, J., *The Theory of Communicative Action*, vol. I: *Reason and the Rationalization of Society*, Heinemann, London, 1984; vol. 2: *Lifeworld and System: A Critique of Functionalist Reason*, Polity, Cambridge, 1987.

Hall, S., 'The Hinterland of Science: Ideology and the "Sociology of Knowledge"', in *On Ideology*, Centre for Contemporary Cultural Studies, Hutchinson, London, 1977.

Hall, S., 'Politics and Ideology: Gramsci', in *On Ideology*, Centre for Contemporary Cultural Studies, Hutchinson, London, 1977.

Halliday, F., 'An Encounter with Fukayama', *New Left Review*, vol. 193, 1992.

Halpern, B., '"Myth" and "Ideology" in Modern Usage', *History and Theory*, vol. 1, 1961.

Hamilton, B., 'The Elements of the Concept of Ideology', *Political Studies*, vol. 35, 1987.

Hanninin, S. and Paldan, L., eds, *Rethinking Ideology: A Marxist Debate*, International General, New York, 1983.

Hansen, P., *Hannah Arendt: Politics, History and Citizenship*, Polity, Cambridge, 1993.

Harding, N., *Lenin's Political Thought*, 2 vols, Macmillan, London, 1977, 1981.

Harvey, D., *The Condition of Postmodernity*, Blackwell, Oxford, 1990.

Head, R., *Ideology and Social Science: Destutt de Tracy and French Liberalism*, Nihoff, Dordrecht, 1982.

Held, D., *Introduction to Critical Theory*, Hutchinson, London, 1980.

Held, D. and Thompson, J., eds, *Habermas: Critical Debates*, Macmillan, London, 1982.

Heller, A. and Feher, F., *The Postmodern Political Condition*, Polity, Cambridge, 1988.

Heywood, A., *Political Ideologies: An Introduction*, Macmillan, Basingstoke, 1992.

Himmelstein, J., *To the Right: The Transformation of American Conservatism*, University of California Press, Berkeley, 1990.

Hirst, P., 'Althusser's Theory of Ideology', *Economy and Society*, vol. 5, 1976.

Hoeveler, J., *Watch on the Right: Conservative Intellectuals in the Reagan Era*, University of Wisconsin Press, Madison, 1991.

Holub, R., *Antonio Gramsci: Beyond Marxism and Postmodernism*, Routledge, New York, 1992.

Horkheimer, M. and Adorno, T., *Dialectic of the Enlightenment*, Herder and Herder, New York, 1972.

Howard, D., *The Politics of Critique*, University of Minnesota Press, Minneapolis, 1989.

Jakubowski, F., *Ideology and Superstructure in Historical Materialism*, Allison and Busby, London, 1976.

Jameson, F., *Postmodernism, or, The Cultural Logic of Late Capitalism*, Verso, London, 1991.

Johnson, H., 'Ideology and the Social System', *International Encyclopaedia of the Social Sciences*, vol. 7, 1968.

Jordan, Z., *The Evolution of Dialectical Materialism*, Macmillan, London, 1967.

Kamuf, P., ed., *A Derrida Reader: Between the Blinds*, Harvester Wheatsheaf, Hemel Hempstead, 1991.

Kaplan, E. and Sprinker, M., eds, *The Althusserian Legacy*, Verso, London, 1993.

Kennedy, E., *Destutt de Tracy and the Origins of 'Ideology'*, American Philosophical Society, Philadelphia, 1978.

Kettler, D., *Mannheim*, Tavistock, London, 1985.

Kolakowski, L., *Modernity on Endless Trial*, University of Chicago Press, Chicago, 1990.

Kress, F. and Hodge, R., *Language as Ideology*, Routledge and Kegan Paul, London, 1979.

Kuhn, T., *The Structure of Scientific Revolutions*, 2nd edn, Chicago University Press, Chicago, 1973.

Lane, R., *Political Ideology*, Free Press of Glencoe, New York, 1962.

Lane, R., 'The Meanings of Ideology', in *Power, Participation and Ideology*, eds C. Larson and P. Wasburn, David McKay, New York, 1969.

LaPalombara, J., 'Decline of Ideology: A Dissent and an Interpretation', *American Political Science Review*, vol. 60, 1966.

Larrain, J., *The Concept of Ideology*, Hutchinson, London, 1979.

Larrain, J., *Marxism and Ideology*, Hutchinson, London, 1983.

Larrain, J., *Ideology and Cultural Identity: Modernity and the Third World Presence*, Polity, Cambridge, 1994.

Leach, E., *Levi-Strauss*, Fontana, London, 1970.

Lee, D., *Competing Discourses: Perspective and Ideology in Language*, Longman, New York, 1992.

Lefebvre, H., *The Sociology of Marx*, Allen Lane, London, 1973.

Lenin, V., *Selected Works*, 3 vols, Foreign Languages Publishing House, Moscow, 1960.

Levi-Strauss, C., *The Savage Mind*, Chicago University Press, Chicago, 1966.

Levi-Strauss, C., *The Raw and the Cooked*, Cape, London, 1970.

Lichtheim, G., *The Concept of Ideology*, Random House, New York, 1967.

Lichtman, R., *Essays in Critical Social Theory: Toward a Marxist Critique of Liberal Ideology*, Peter Lang, San Francisco, 1994.

Lipset, S., *Political Man*, Heinemann, London, 1960.

Loader, C., *The Intellectual Development of Karl Mannheim: Culture, Politics and Planning*, Cambridge University Press, Cambridge, 1985.

Lukacs, G., *History and Class Consciousness*, Merlin Press, London, 1971.

Lukes, S., *Power: A Radical Analysis*, Macmillan, London, 1974.

Lyotard, J.F., *The Postmodern Condition: A Report on Knowledge*, University of Minnesota Press, Minneapolis, 1984.

McCarney, J., *The Real World of Ideology*, Harvester, Brighton, 1980.

McCarney, J., 'Shaping Ends: Reflections on Fukayama', *New Left Review*, vol. 202, 1993.

McDonald, L., 'Myth, Politics and Political Science', *Western Political Quarterly*, vol. 22, 1969.

McDonagh, R., 'Ideology and False Consciousness: Lukacs', in *On Ideology*, Centre for Contemporary Cultural Studies, Hutchinson, London, 1977.

McLellan, D., *Marxism after Marx*, Macmillan, London, 1980.

McLennan, G., 'Althusser's Theory of Ideology' in *On Ideology*, Centre for Contemporary Cultural Studies, Hutchinson, London, 1977.

McMurtry, J., *The Structure of Marx's World-View*, Princeton University Press, Princeton, 1978.

Malachowski, A., ed., *Reading Rorty*, Blackwell, Oxford, 1990.

Mannheim, K., *Ideology and Utopia*, Routledge and Kegan Paul, London, 1936.

Mannheim, K., *From Karl Mannheim*, ed. K. Wolff, Oxford University Press, New York, 1971.

Manning, D., ed., *The Form of Ideology*, Allen and Unwin, London, 1980.

Marcuse, H., *One-Dimensional Man*, Routledge and Kegan Paul, London, 1964.

Marx, K., *Selected Writings*, ed. D. McLellan, Oxford University Press, Oxford, 1977.

Marx, K., *Capital: An Abridged Version*, Oxford University Press, Oxford, 1995.

Mepham, J., 'The Theory of Ideology in *Capital*', in *Issues in Marxist Philosophy*, eds J. Mepham and D.H. Ruben, Harvester, Hassocks, 1979.

Merquior, J., *From Prague to Paris: A Critique of Structuralist and Post-Structuralist Thought*, Verso, London, 1986.

Merton, R., *Social Theory and Social Structure*, Free Press, Glencoe, New York, 1957.

Meszaros, I., *The Power of Ideology*, Harvester Wheatsheaf, Hemel Hempstead, 1989.

Mills, C., '"Ideology" in Marx and Engels', *Philosophical Forum*, vol. 16, 1985.

Minogue, K., *Alien Powers: The Pure Theory of Ideology*, Weidenfeld and Nicolson, London, 1985.

Mitchell, W., *Iconology: Image, Text, Ideology*, University of Chicago Press, Chicago, 1986.

Mouffe, C., 'Hegemony and Ideology in Gramsci', in *Gramsci and Marxist Theory*, ed. C. Mouffe, Routledge and Kegan Paul, London, 1979.

Mullins, W., 'On the Concept of Ideology in Political Science', *American Political Science Review*, vol. 66, 1972.

Mullins, W., 'Sartori's Concept of Ideology: A Dissent and an Alternative', in *Public Opinion and Political Attitudes: A Reader*, ed. A. Wilcox, Wiley, New York, 1974.

Naess, A. *et al.*, *Democracy, Ideology and Objectivity*, Blackwell, Oxford, 1956.

Nelson, C. and Grossberg, L., *Marxism and the Interpretation of Culture*, Macmillan, London, 1988.

Neu, J., ed., *The Cambridge Companion to Freud*, Cambridge University Press, Cambridge, 1991.

Oakeshott, M., *Rationalism in Politics and Other Essays*, Methuen, London, 1962.

Outhwaite, W., *Habermas: An Introduction*, Polity, Cambridge, 1994.

Parekh, B., *Marx's Theory of Ideology*, Croom Helm, London, 1982.

Pareto, V., *Sociological Writings*, ed. S. Finer, Pall Mall Press, London, 1966.

Parkin, F., *Weber*, Ellis Horwood, Chichester, 1982.

Peffer, R., *Marxism, Morality and Social Justice*, Princeton University Press, Princeton, 1990.

Perez-Diaz, V., *The Return of Civil Society*, London, 1993.

Perkins, S., *Marxism and the Proletariat: A Lukacsian Perspective*, Pluto, London, 1993.

Plamenatz, J., *Ideology*, Macmillan, London, 1970.

Putnam, R., 'Studying Elite Political Culture: The Case of Ideology', *American Political Science Review*, vol. 65, 1971.

Reich, W., *The Mass Psychology of Fascism*, Penguin, Harmondsworth, 1975.

Remmling, G., *The Sociology of Karl Mannheim*, Routledge and Kegan Paul, London, 1975.

Resch, R., *Althusser and the Renewal of Marxist Social Theory*, University of California Press, Berkeley, 1992.

Ricoeur, P., *Hermeneutics and the Human Sciences*, Cambridge University Press, Cambridge, 1981.

Ricoeur, P., *Lectures on Ideology and Utopia*, Columbia University Press, New York, 1986.

Roazen, P., *Freud: Social and Political Thought*, Hogarth Press, London, 1968.

Rorty, R., *Contingency, Irony and Solidarity*, Cambridge University Press, Cambridge, 1989.

Rose, M., *The Post-modern and the Post-industrial: A Critical Analysis*, Cambridge University Press, Cambridge, 1991.

Rossi-Landi, F., *Marxism and Ideology*, Clarendon Press, Oxford, 1990.

Rustin, M., 'No exit from Capitalism?', *New Left Review*, vol. 193, 1992.

Sartori, G., 'Politics, Ideology and Belief Systems', *American Political Science Review*, vol. 63, 1969.

Scott, P., *Religion, Ideology and Theology*, Cambridge University Press, Cambridge, 1994.

Seliger, M., *Ideology and Politics*, Allen and Unwin, London, 1976.

Seliger, M., *The Marxist Conception of Ideology*, Allen and Unwin, London, 1977.

Shaw, W., 'Ruling Ideas', in *Analyzing Marxism*, eds R. Ware and K. Nielsen, University of Calgary Press, Calgary, 1989

Shils, E., 'The Concept and Function of Ideology', *International Encyclopaedia of the Social Sciences*, vol. 7, 1968.

Shtromas, A., *The End of 'Isms'?: Reflections on the Fate of Ideological Politics after Communism's Collapse*, Blackwell, Oxford, 1993.

Simonds, A., *Karl Mannheim's Sociology of Knowledge*, Clarendon Press, Oxford, 1978.

Simons, H. and Billig, M., eds., *After Postmodernism: Reconstructing Ideology Critique*, Sage, London, 1994.

Spurling, L., ed., *Sigmund Freud: Critical Assessments*, Routledge, New York, vol. 3, 1989.

Sturrock, J., ed., *Structuralism and Since*, Oxford University Press, Oxford, 1979.

Taylor, C., 'Neutrality in Political Science', in *Philosophy, Politics and Society*, eds P. Laslett and W. Runciman, Blackwell, Oxford, 1967.

Taylor, C., *Sources of the Self: The Making of the Modern Identity*, Cambridge University Press, Cambridge, 1985.

Therborn, G., *The Ideology of Power and The Power of Ideology*, Verso, London, 1980.

Thompson, J., *Studies in the Theory of Ideology*, Polity Press, Cambridge, 1984.

Turner, B., *Max Weber: From History to Modernity*, Routledge, New York, 1992.

Turner, D., *Marxism and Christianity*, Blackwell, Oxford, 1983.

Turner, S., ed., *Emile Durkheim: Sociologist and Moralist*, Routledge, New York, 1993.

Vincent, A., *Modern Political Ideologies*, Blackwell, Oxford, 1992.

Vincent, A., 'British Conservatism and the Problem of Ideology', *Political Studies*, vol. 42, 1994.

Wagner, P., *A Sociology of Modernity: Liberty and Discipline*, Routledge, New York, 1994.

Waxman, C., *The End of Ideology Debate*, Funk and Wagnall, New York, 1968.

Weber, M., *The Protestant Ethic and the Spirit of Capitalism*, ed. A. Giddens, Allen and Unwin, London, 1976.

Welch, C., *Liberty and Utility: The French Ideologues and the Transformation of Liberalism*, Columbia University Press, New York, 1984.

White, S., *The Recent Work of Jürgen Habermas: Reason, Justice and Modernity*, Cambridge University Press, Cambridge, 1988.

White, S., *Political Theory and Postmodernism*, Cambridge University Press, Cambridge, 1991.

Williams, H., *Concepts of Ideology*, Wheatsheaf, Brighton, 1988.

Williams, R., *Marxism and Literature*, Oxford University Press, Oxford, 1977.

Zizek, S., *The Sublime Object of Ideology*, Verso, London, 1989.

Index